"HEART SPEAKS TO HEART"

To Saint John Henry Newman

*To the Seminarians, Students, Faculty, Staff
and Board of Trustees of St. Joseph's Seminary, Dunwoodie*

"HEART SPEAKS TO HEART"

SAINT JOHN HENRY NEWMAN AND THE CALL TO HOLINESS

EDITED BY

Kevin J. O'Reilly

with a foreword by Timothy Cardinal Dolan

GRACEWING

First published in England in 2021
by
Gracewing
2 Southern Avenue
Leominster
Herefordshire HR6 0QF
United Kingdom
www.gracewing.co.uk

All rights reserved

No part of this publication may be reproduced,
stored in a retrieval system, or transmitted in any
form or by any means, electronic, mechanical,
photocopying, recording or otherwise,
without the written permission of the publisher.

Compilation and editorial material
© 2021, Saint Joseph's Seminary, Dunwoodie

The rights of the editor and contributors
to be identified as the authors of this work
have been asserted in accordance with
the Copyright, Designs and Patents Act 1988.

The publishers have no responsibility
for the persistence or accuracy of URLs for websites
referred to in this publication, and do not guarantee
that any content on such websites is, or will remain,
accurate or appropriate.

ISBN 978 085244 963 9

Typeset by Word and Page, Chester, UK

Cover design by Bernardita Peña Hurtado

Contents

Foreword	vii
Timothy Cardinal Dolan	
Introduction	xv
Contributors	xix
1. The Significance of Newman's Canonization	1
Ian Ker	
2. Homily: The Commemoration of All the Faithful Departed	11
Bishop John Barres	
3. Saint John Henry Cardinal Newman and the Standard of Holiness	17
Edward Short	
4. Newman and the Italians: How Italy and her People Brought Newman to a New Holiness	39
Jo Anne Cammarata Sylva	
5. "The Value of One Single Soul": Newman on the Gravity of Sin and the Quality of Mercy	57
Ryan Marr	
6. To Witness the Unseen: Sanctity in the Thought of John Henry Newman and Wilfrid Ward	69
Elizabeth Huddleston	
7. St. John Henry Newman and the Ventures of Faith	93
Christopher Blum	
8. "Until Christ Be Formed in You" (Gal 4:19): Saint John Henry Newman's Theological-Pastoral Mystagogy	103
Robert P. Imbelli	
9. Newman and Apologetics	125
Kevin J. O'Reilly	
10. Epilogue	155
Bishop James Massa	
Index	159

Requiescat in Pace

Father Kevin O'Reilly
1969–2021

This book was in his final days a labor of love.
Now he knows the One in whom he believed. (2 Tim 1:12)

Foreword

Timothy Michael Cardinal Dolan
Archbishop of New York

In August of 1826, in his magnificent sermon "Holiness Necessary for Future Blessedness," St. John Henry Newman reflected upon what "is declared in one form or another in every part of Scripture":[1] our need for holiness and how we are made holy. For Newman, to make sinful creatures holy was "the great end which our Lord had in view in taking upon Him our nature" and the necessity of holiness for salvation is clearly evident throughout salvation history. Consequently, Newman established holiness and calling others to it as among the central themes of his life, preaching, and writings.

Commenting on Hebrews 12:14 ("Holiness, without which no man shall see the Lord"), Newman analyzes the questions that naturally arise upon consideration of the verse's insistence upon personal holiness as necessary for salvation, and in doing so identifies the various dimensions of sanctity for which Scripture inspires us all to strive:

> Now, someone may ask, "Why is it that holiness is a necessary qualification for our being received into heaven? Why is it that the Bible enjoins upon us so strictly to love, fear, and obey God, to be just, honest, meek, pure in heart, forgiving, heavenly-minded, self-denying, humble, and resigned? Man is confessedly weak and corrupt; why then is he enjoined to be so religious, so unearthly? Why is he required (in the strong language of Scripture) to become 'a new creature'? Since he is by nature what he is, would it not be an act of greater mercy in God to save him altogether without this holiness, which it is so difficult, yet (as it appears) so necessary to possess?"[2]

---

[1] John Henry Newman, "Holiness Necessary for Future Blessedness," in *Parochial and Plain Sermons* (London: Longman, Green & Co., 1917), I, sermon 1, 1.
[2] Ibid., 1–2.

"Heart Speaks to Heart"

Thus, according to the Bible and Newman, to "love, fear and obey God," "to be just, honest, meek, pure in heart, forgiving, heavenly-minded, self-denying, humble, and resigned" and "to become a new creature" are the qualities that comprise holiness and are required for each person to enter heaven.

But why can only the holy enter eternal life? Why should we deny ourselves in this world and make every effort to prepare ourselves for the next? Newman states his answer with characteristic clarity: "That, even supposing a man of unholy life were suffered to enter heaven, *he would not be happy there;* so that it would be no mercy to permit him to enter."[3] Heaven can be a place of happiness only to those who are holy, because heaven is where we adore, worship and enjoy the loving presence of the Triune God forever. Such a place is not for anyone who pursues their own desires, but only for those who love and seek God alone. Without personal holiness, any individual in heaven would find eternity in the presence of God to be unbearable. So, holiness is necessary, because "heaven would be hell to an irreligious man."[4]

Thereafter, Newman, like every great homilist, explicates what this means for his audience and gives practical advice on how to grow in holiness. First, he affirms that "holiness is prescribed to us as the condition on our part for admission into heaven" and bids us to make holiness our life's goal. Then, he outlines how to do this: namely, to respond to God's grace by putting our faith into action through good works. This is not because our deeds "earn" God's love, but rather that they develop the interior habits and frame of mind that characterize holiness:

> Good works (as they are called) are required, not as if they had any thing of merit in them, not as if they could of themselves turn away God's anger for our sins, or purchase heaven for us, but because they are the means, under God's grace, of strengthening and showing forth that holy principle which God implants in the heart, and without which (as the text tells us) we cannot see Him. The more numerous are our acts of charity, self-denial, and forbearance, of course the more will our minds be schooled into a charitable, self-denying, and forbearing temper. The more frequent are our prayers, the more humble, patient and religious are our daily deeds, this communion with God, these

---

[3] *Ibid.*, 3 (emphasis in original).
[4] *Ibid.*, 7.

> holy works, will be the means of making our hearts holy, and
> of preparing us for the future presence of God.[5]

For Newman, all people (clergy and laity alike) are called to holiness through humble acts of virtue and service, which progressively prepare us to enter the presence of God.

However, this cannot happen overnight; it is the task of a lifetime. Our life's work in this world, therefore, must be focused upon loving and serving God and advancing in holiness, which is "the result of many patient, repeated efforts after obedience, gradually working on us, and first modifying and then changing our hearts." There is no salvation without holiness. In light of this, Newman challenges his congregation: "Be you content with nothing short of perfection; exert yourselves day by day to grow in knowledge and grace; that, if so be, you may at length attain to the presence of Almighty God."[6]

In conclusion, so that people do not get discouraged in facing this demanding and seemingly impossible task, he inspires us never to give up, because it is ultimately God who is our strength and will make our holiness like His own:

> Lastly, while we labour to mould our hearts after the pattern of holiness of our Heavenly Father, it is our comfort to know ... that we are not left to ourselves, but that the Holy Ghost is graciously present with us, and enables us to triumph over, and to change our minds. It is a comfort and an encouragement, while it is an anxious and awful thing, to know that God works in and through us. We are the instruments, but we are only the instruments, of our own salvation. Let no one say that I discourage him, and propose to him a task beyond his strength. All of us have the gifts of grace pledged to us from our youth up ... Narrow, indeed, is the way of life, but infinite is His love and power who is with the Church, in Christ's place, to guide us along it.[7]

By humbly submitting to God and His grace and endeavoring to serve Him with our whole being, we, His instruments, will be truly sanctified by God and grow in His likeness.

---

[5] Ibid., 9.
[6] Ibid., 13.
[7] Ibid., 13–14.

"Heart Speaks to Heart"

The topic of holiness is so central to Newman's life and thought that it is no surprise that he selected this masterpiece as the opening sermon in his first published volume of sermons in 1834, a collection which would become his influential *Parochial and Plain Sermons*, one of the great classics of Christian spirituality. In fact, according to Louis Bouyer, even the title of the sermon "may be taken as the program not only of all of his subsequent preachings but of all that will constitute his later theological work … It may be said that this sermon gives us the key to all that follows."[8] Since his initial spiritual conversion as a teenager, particularly after reading Thomas Scott's autobiography *The Force of Truth*, he had made two of Scott's maxims his own: "Holiness rather than peace" and "Growth the only evidence of Life."[9] It was his striving towards growth in holiness that led him to the Oxford Movement and eventually to leave the Anglican Church and to be received into the Roman Catholic Church.

Newman himself, despite his life-long personal efforts to be holy, repeatedly denied being a saint in his own lifetime. Thanks be to God that the Holy Spirit had the final say on that question! Nevertheless, in his famous *Biglietto* speech in Rome upon receiving the official letter that Pope Leo XIII had named him a cardinal on May 12, 1879, Newman humbly averred that "in a long course of years I have made many mistakes. I have nothing of that high perfection which belongs to the writings of Saints, viz., that error cannot be found in them."[10] However, he never deterred from encouraging all people to be saints in their daily lives. Indeed, he often stressed that sainthood does not require anything extraordinary, but rather the performance of our everyday tasks well and with a pure heart. For example, in his "A Short Road to Perfection," composed in 1856, Newman states directly what we must do to be holy and perfect:

> If you ask me what you are to do in order to be perfect, I say, first—Do not lie in bed beyond the due time of rising; give your first thoughts to God; make a good visit to the Blessed Sacrament; say the Angelus devoutly; eat and drink to God's glory; say the Rosary well; be recollected; keep out bad thoughts; make your

---

[8] Louis Bouyer, *Newman's Vision of Faith* (San Francisco: Ignatius Press, 1986), 19.
[9] John Henry Newman, *Apologia pro Vita Sua* (London: Longmans, Green & Co., 1908), 4.
[10] John Henry Newman, "Biglietto Speech," in John T. Ford, ed., *John Henry Newman: Spiritual Writings* (Maryknoll, NY: Orbis Books, 2012), 221–2.

evening meditation well; examine yourself daily; go to bed in good time, and you are already perfect.[11]

Splendid advice, even for our busy lives today!

Recent popes have celebrated Newman's sanctity and have held him up as an example for us to follow. Pope St. John Paul the Great, in honor of the bicentennial of Newman's birth, wrote to the Archbishop of Birmingham and prayed "that the time will soon come when the Church can officially and publicly proclaim the exemplary holiness of Cardinal John Henry Newman, one of the most distinguished and versatile champions of English spirituality."[12] This prayer was answered on October 13, 2019, when Pope Francis declared Newman a saint and, in his homily during the Mass of Canonization, praised Newman for his holiness and his exemplary description of what sanctity entails:

> Such is the holiness of daily life, which Saint John Henry Newman described in these words: "The Christian has a deep, silent, hidden peace, which the world sees not … The Christian is cheerful, easy, kind, gentle, courteous, candid, unassuming, has no pretense … with so little that is unusual or striking in his bearing, that he may easily be taken at first sight for an ordinary man (*Parochial and Plain Sermons*, V, 5). Let us ask to be like that, "kindly lights" amid the encircling gloom. Jesus, "stay with me, and then I shall begin to shine as Thou shinest: so to shine as to be a light to others" (*Meditations on Christian Doctrine*, VII, 3). Amen.[13]

Now, as a saint of the Catholic Church, Cardinal Newman intercedes for us as we strive for daily holiness.

In honor of Newman's canonization, St. Joseph's Seminary, Dunwoodie, in Yonkers, New York, hosted a symposium of Newman scholars on November 1–2, 2019, entitled *"Cor ad Cor Loquitur*: St. John Henry Newman and the Call to Holiness." This colloquium included such noted Newman experts as Fr. Ian Ker, Edward Short and numerous others, who, inspired by Newman's long-awaited

---

[11] John Henry Newman, "A Short Road to Perfection," in *Meditations and Devotions* (New York: Longmans, Green & Co., 1907), 285–6.

[12] Pope John Paul II, "Letter to Archbishop Vincent Nichols: Newman Belongs to Every Time and People," *L'Osservatore Romano*, English edition, March 7, 2001.

[13] Pope Francis, "Homily of His Holiness Pope Francis," *Bulletin of the Holy See Press Office*, October 13, 2019.

"Heart Speaks to Heart"

sainthood, presented fascinating papers which reflected on his life, legacy and different aspects of his understanding of holiness and his summons for all of us to pursue holy lives.

The volume which you now hold in your hands is the fruit of this labor of love. In it, Fr. Ker outlines how Newman is in many ways a saint for our times, anticipated many of the themes of the Second Vatican Council and can guide us in interpreting both the Council documents and the post-Conciliar period. My brother Bishop, Bishop John Barres of Rockville Centre, New York, presents an inspiring homily in which he describes how his parents, inspired by Newman's writings, converted to Catholicism and encourages us to look to Newman as a model for holiness and evangelization. Edward Short explicates how Newman insists upon personal holiness for all and challenges, encourages and inspires us to be holy by his own life and works. Other articles treat how Newman's early voyage to Italy introduced him to many aspects of Catholic tradition and spirituality and inspired him throughout his life, his understanding of holiness as radical separation from sin, and how sanctity stems from the realization of the presence of the invisible divine world by our imagination and conscience. In addition, you will find papers which cover Newman's invitation for all to accept Christian faith as a radical commitment, his pastoral mystagogy which links theology, spirituality and pastoral ministry, and his understanding of apologetics.

I am grateful to the Board of Trustees, faculty, seminarians and students of St. Joseph's Seminary for organizing and attending this symposium and I thank all of the scholars for the hard work that has resulted in this book. All of these presentations are seeped with love for Newman the saint and his inspiring example for us to strive for holiness. I am sure that you will find this collection to be a valuable contribution to contemporary study of Newman's thought, as well as intellectually stimulating and spiritually edifying.

Two days after his *Biglietto* speech, on May 14, 1879, Cardinal Newman went to the English College in Rome and was presented with a set of vestments embroidered with his cardinalatial coat of arms from the English-speaking Catholics in Rome. At the ceremony, Lady Herbert of Lea summed up the love and admiration of the assembled crowd by addressing Newman thus:

Foreword

> We feel that in making you a Cardinal the Holy Father has not only given public testimony of his appreciation of your great merits and of the value of your admirable writings in defense of God and His Church, but has also conferred the greatest possible honour on all English-speaking Catholics, who have long looked up to you as their spiritual father and their guide in the paths of holiness.[14]

Almost a century and a half later, these same words can also express the joy of the whole Church today who similarly rejoice in Newman's canonization. May St. John Henry Newman always be our spiritual father and guide us to holiness and eternal life!

---

[14] W. P. Neville, ed., *Addresses to Cardinal Newman with his Replies* (New York: Longmans, Green & Co., 1905), 72.

Introduction

On September 19, 2010, Pope Benedict XVI, during his homily at the Mass of the Beatification of John Henry Cardinal Newman in Birmingham, England, enumerated many of Newman's various accomplishments and impressive contributions to the life of the Church, including his intellectual gifts, priestly ministry and his "prolific pen." In particular, the Holy Father praised Newman for his insights into humanity's vocation to holiness and our desire for communion with God:

> Cardinal Newman's motto, *Cor ad cor loquitur,* or "Heart speaks to heart," gives us an insight into his understanding of the Christian life as a call to holiness, experienced as the profound desire of the human heart to enter into intimate communion with the Heart of God. He reminds us that faithfulness to prayer gradually transforms us into the divine likeness. As he wrote in one of his many fine sermons, "a habit of prayer, the practice of turning to God and the unseen world in every season, in every place, in every emergency — prayer, I say, has what may be called a natural effect in spiritualizing and elevating the soul. A man is no longer what he was before; gradually ... he has imbibed a new set of ideas, and become imbued with fresh principles" (*Parochial and Plain Sermons*, IV, 230–1).[1]

Newman's cardinalatial motto was highlighted as encapsulating not only his own personal life of holiness, but also what human life itself is all about: responding to the call to holiness from God's own heart through offering our hearts and entire selves to God in prayer and service.

Upon receiving the joyful announcement on July 1, 2019 that Pope Francis would canonize Cardinal Newman on October 13, 2019, the administration and faculty of St. Joseph's Seminary, Dunwoodie, in Yonkers, New York, decided to mark the momentous occasion by hosting a symposium of noted Newman scholars

---

[1] Pope Benedict XVI, "Beatification Homily: Benedict XVI," in John T. Ford, ed., *John Henry Newman: Spiritual Writings* (Marynoll, NY: Orbis Books, 2012), 231.

in order to explore the various historical, theological and pastoral dimensions of Newman's understanding of the universal call to holiness. Given the Seminary's mission of forming future priests as well as candidates for the Permanent Diaconate, lay people and religious, the intention was that this colloquium dedicated to Newman's sainthood and his conception of humanity's vocation to sanctity would serve as an inspiration to the Seminary community and the entire local Catholic Church in the downstate New York region.

The call for papers was issued over the summer and many leaders in the field of Newman studies responded immediately and committed to participate, most notably Fr. Ian Ker, generally considered the most prominent and respected living Newman scholar, who agreed to travel to New York and deliver the keynote address. The Symposium was held on November 1st and 2nd at Dunwoodie, with the noted author Edward Short offering the opening address over dinner on the Solemnity of All Saints. The following day, All Souls' Day, was highlighted by the Holy Sacrifice of the Mass with Bishop John Barres of Rockville Centre as celebrant and homilist, Fr. Ker's talk and various small group presentations by Newman experts addressing his contributions on such important topics as holiness, vocation, faith, conscience, sin, mercy, mystagogy, and apologetics. The symposium attracted attendees from far and wide and was greatly enjoyed and appreciated by all.

This book includes many of the papers presented during the symposium, and it is hoped that it will provide much food for thought and reflection for scholars, clergy, lay people and all those interested in and inspired by the life and thought of St. John Henry Newman.

The Newman Symposium and this book were true labors of love and the result of the hard work and dedication of many people. First and foremost, special thanks are owed to the Bishops of the Borromeo Council: Timothy Cardinal Dolan of the Archdiocese of New York, Bishop Nicholas DiMarzio of the Diocese of Brooklyn, and Bishop John Barres of the Diocese of Rockville Centre for their ongoing support of the mission of St. Joseph's Seminary and the Newman Symposium in particular. Especially, we thank Cardinal Dolan for contributing the Foreword to this book and Bishop Barres for his inspiring homily (also included in this book), his promotion of Cardinal Newman in his diocese, and for bringing a large contingent of attendees to the symposium from Rockville Centre.

Introduction

No one deserves more credit for the success of the Newman Symposium than Msgr. Peter Vaccari, former Rector of St. Joseph's Seminary, who is currently the President of the Catholic Near East Welfare Association. As Rector, Msgr. Vaccari worked tirelessly in arranging for the speakers and the massive amount of details connected with running such an elaborate event and he deserves our profound gratitude. In these various tasks, he was admirably assisted by Mary Broglie, Cynthia Harrison, Danielle Pizzola and the entire Seminary staff and we thank all for their hard work. We also acknowledge and appreciate the Seminary Board of Trustees and Faculty for their presence at and support of the symposium.

Msgr. Vaccari also strongly advocated for this book project to commemorate the symposium and Fr. William Cleary, who served as interim Rector and is presently Vice-Rector, and Bishop James Massa, the new Rector of St. Joseph's Seminary, who has graciously written an Epilogue to the book, also have been unwavering in their support and all merit our recognition and appreciation.

The symposium would not have been possible without our impressive lineup of speakers, all of whom demonstrated their hard work and expertise in their well-crafted talks. Headlined by Fr. Ian Ker, the roster of speakers included Fr. Nicholas Becker, Christopher Blum, Jo Anne Cammarata Sylva, Robert Christie, Sr. Kathleen Dietz, Elizabeth Huddleston, Fr. Robert Imbelli, Ryan Marr, Fr. Kevin O'Reilly, and Edward Short. The entire Seminary community is indebted to them for their participation and scholarship.

This book was a collaborative effort, guided by Tom Longford, Fr. Paul Haffner and the staff of Gracewing Publishing. Their patience and wisdom in making this book a reality were both impressive and greatly appreciated. Special thanks to Edward Short for helping us make contact with Gracewing Publishing and to Connor Flatz, the Director of the Corrigan Memorial Library of St. Joseph's Seminary, for tracking down some essential references.

At the conclusion of his homily at the Mass of Beatification in 2010, Pope Benedict cited the following lines from Cardinal Newman's *Dream of Gerontius* to offer praise and thanksgiving to God for His gift of John Henry Newman to the Church:

> *Praise to the Holiest in the height*
> *And in the depth be praise;*

"Heart Speaks to Heart"

In all his words most wonderful,
Most sure in all his ways![2]

May these words be our prayer as we glorify God for the canonization of St. John Henry Newman! God personally calls all of us to lead holy lives and St. John Henry Newman's exemplary life, holiness, thought, and writings are a model of how we are to respond lovingly to this invitation.

This collection of papers in honor of Cardinal Newman's sainthood, it is hoped, will be a lasting contribution to current Newman scholarship and, in line with his cardinalatial motto "Heart speaks to heart," will inspire us to hear and answer God's call from the depths of our hearts with our own personal holiness and to invite others to do the same, one heart at a time.

---

[2] John Henry Newman, *Dream of Gerontius*, in *Verses on Various Occasions* (London: Longmans, Green & Co., 1903), 363.

Contributors

Bishop **John O. Barres**, D.D., S.T.D., is the Bishop of the Diocese of Rockville Centre. He holds degrees from Princeton University, New York University, the Catholic University of America and the Pontifical University of the Holy Cross in Rome.

Dr. **Christopher O. Blum**, Ph.D., is the Academic Dean and Professor of History and Philosophy at the Augustine Institute in Denver, Colorado. He is the author, translator and editor of numerous books and articles, including *Critics of the Enlightenment: Readings in the French Counter-Revolutionary Tradition* (2004) and *True Reformers* (2017).

Dr. **Jo Anne Cammarata Sylva**, D.Litt., is Professor of Humanities at Assumption College for Sisters and holds a doctorate from Drew University. She is the author of *How Italy and her People Shaped Cardinal Newman: Italian Influences on an English Mind* (2010).

Timothy Michael Cardinal Dolan, D.D., Ph.D., is the Archbishop of New York. He holds a doctorate in Church History from the Catholic University of America and is the author of many books on history, theology and spirituality.

Dr. **Elizabeth Huddleston**, Ph.D., is the Coordinator of Research for the National Institute of Newman Studies (NINS), located in Pittsburgh, Pennsylvania. She is also the Managing Editor of the *Newman Studies Journal*, which is managed by NINS and published by the Catholic University of America Press. Elizabeth received her doctorate in theology from the University of Dayton. Her research interests include the theology of and reception of John Henry Newman, the relationship between music and theology, ecumenical and interfaith conversations, and the intersection of dogmatic/doctrinal theology with Christian mysticism.

Fr. **Robert Imbelli**, Ph.D., is a priest of the Archdiocese of New York and Associate Professor Emeritus of Theology at Boston College. He is the author of numerous articles and books, including the prize-winning *Handing on the Faith: The Church's Mission and Challenge* (2006) and *Rekindling the Christic Imagination: Theological Meditations for the New Evangelization* (2014).

Fr. **Ian Ker** is a professor at Oxford University and is widely regarded as the world's foremost scholar on John Henry Newman. He has written over twenty books on Newman, including what is universally considered the definitive biography on Newman: *John Henry Newman: A Biography* (1988, 2nd edn 2009).

Dr. **Ryan J. Marr**, Ph.D., is the Director of the National Institute for Newman Studies and the Associate Editor of the Journal *Newman Studies*. He is the author of *To Be Perfect is to Have Changed Often: The Development of John Henry Newman's Ecclesiological Outlook (1845–1877)* (2018) and has contributed essays to numerous books on Newman, including the *Oxford Handbook of John Henry Newman* (2018).

Bishop **James Massa**, D.D., Ph.D., is an Auxiliary Bishop of the Diocese of Brooklyn and the Rector of Saint Joseph's Seminary, Dunwoodie. He holds a doctorate in systematic theology from Fordham University, has written widely on topics related to the sacraments, Christian unity and the Church's engagement with Judaism and other religions, and has served as the Executive Director of the Secretariat for Ecumenical and Interreligious Affairs at the United States Conference of Catholic Bishops.

Fr. **Kevin J. O'Reilly**, S.T.D., a priest of the Archdiocese of New York, served as the Academic Dean and Professor of Dogmatic Theology at St. Joseph's Seminary, Dunwoodie. He held a doctorate in dogmatic theology from the Pontifical Gregorian University in Rome. Fr Kevin died during a snowstorm in the Bronx on 1 February 2021 while in the course of his priestly duties.

Edward Short is the author of *Newman and History* (2017), *Newman and his Family* (2013), and *Newman and his Contemporaries* (2011). His critical edition of the first volume of *Difficulties of Anglicans* is published by Gracewing (2021) in its Millennium Edition of Newman's works. He lives in New York with his wife and two young children.

1

The Significance of Newman's Canonization

Ian Ker

THE SIGNIFICANCE OF NEWMAN'S CANONIZATION is that it opens the way for him to be declared a Doctor of the Church. I believe that, just as St. Robert Bellarmine is the Doctor of the Tridentine Church, so St. John Henry Newman will come to be seen as the Doctor of the post-Vatican II Church.

The first volume of the Library of the Fathers, which Newman and Pusey had initiated, was published in 1838. Slightly more than a hundred years later, in 1942, the French theologians Henri de Lubac and Jean Daniélou began publishing the series *Sources Chrétiennes*.

There is only one text in the documents of Vatican II that can be attributed directly to Newman: the reference to the development of doctrine in the Dogmatic Constitution on Divine Revelation *Dei Verbum*. But he anticipated several other documents, notably the Dogmatic Constitution on the Church *Lumen Gentium*, surely the most important document of a Council almost entirely concerned with the Church. Its first two chapters define what the Council understood to be the Church, and the underlying theology is entirely Scriptural and Patristic, exactly the same theology that Newman had imbibed from his systematic reading of the Greek Fathers which he undertook on being deprived of his tutorship at Oriel College, Oxford.

In his lack of support for Pope Pius IX's notorious *Syllabus of Errors* (1864), which insisted on the temporal power of the papacy and condemned progress and political liberalism, Newman also anticipated Vatican II's Pastoral Constitution on the Church in the

"Heart Speaks to Heart"

Modern World *Gaudium et Spes*, which abandoned the Church's old defensive negativity towards the world. Again, Newman's insistence on the importance of the laity in a highly clericalized Church looks forward to Vatican II's Decree on the Apostolate of the Laity *Apostolicam Actuositatem*. His encouragement of ecumenical initiatives foreshadows Vatican II's Decree on Ecumenism *Unitatis Redintegratio*.

Newman's writings also provide a hermeneutic for a balanced interpretation of the Vatican II texts. As a theologian who was both very radical but also at the same time very traditional, he held the same kind of theology of non-Christian religions that we find in the Council's Declaration on the Relation of the Church to non-Christian religions *Nostra Aetate*. He is more radical than the Council in speaking not only of the good and the truth to be found in non-Christian religions, but also of even referring to the "Dispensation of Paganism,"[1] with its implicit reference to an actual covenant, and in advocating that Christian missionaries should not only purify what is good and true in non-Christian religions, but even base their preaching of the Gospel on such elements. However, the kind of religious pluralism that arose after the Council, in which Christianity was seen as merely one of many valid religious, would have been utterly rejected by Newman, who was in no doubt that Christ alone was the Redeemer.

In what has become a famous speech, Pope Benedict XVI, in 2005, contrasted two rival interpretations of the Second Vatican Council. On the one hand, there was an interpretation that he would call a "hermeneutic of discontinuity and rupture"; on the other hand, there was a "hermeneutic of reform," or a renewal that was in continuity rather than rupture. Newman had made exactly the same point in his *Essay on the Development of Christian Doctrine*, when he wrote that Christianity "changes" not in order to be different, but "in order to remain the same," a progress which Newman called "development" as opposed to corruption.

There can be no doubt but that Newman would have been with the reformers rather than the conservatives at Vatican II, but with the moderate reformers and not the extreme reformers who sought a rupture with the Church's tradition, a break with the past. And

---

[1] See John Henry Newman, *The Arians of the Fourth Century* (London: Longmans, Green & Co., 1908), 81.

he would have interpreted the documents of the Council in the light of the mini-theology of Councils which he adumbrated in private letters before, during, and after the First Vatican Council. The first consideration that struck Newnan was that Councils move "alternately in contrary directions." In the early Councils, doctrines "were not struck off all at once but piecemeal—one Council did one thing, another a second—and so the whole dogma was built up." It was because "the first portion of it looked extreme" that controversies arose which led to subsequent Councils that *"explained* and *completed* what was first done."[2] Thus, the Council of Chalcedon had completed the definition of the preceding Council of Ephesus, just as the Second Vatican Council completed the teaching of the First Vatican Council on the papacy with a much fuller teaching on the Church. This historical perspective might have given pause to those liberal Catholics who were expecting and hoping for another Council which would fully implement the so-called "spirit of Vatican II" in clearer and more categorical terms.

The history of the early Church showed Newman only too graphically how confusion and dissension inevitably followed a Council, and so the turbulent aftermath of Vatican II would hardly have surprised him. For Councils, he saw, "generally acted as a lever displacing and disordering portions of the existing theological system," leading to acrimonious controversy. After Vatican I, it should hardly have been unexpected that a faction of the Church would leave in protest to form the Old Catholic Church, while the extreme Ultramontanes were naturally to take every opportunity to exaggerate Vatican I's very moderate definition of papal infallibility. Newman would not have been in the least surprised by either the Lefebvrist schism or by those theologians who after Vatican II constantly invoked the so-called "spirit of Vatican II" to "supplement" the actual documents of the Council. It suited both protagonists so to exaggerate the conciliar texts as to pervert what was actually change-in-continuity, that is development, into revolutionary rupture.

At the beginning of his *Essay on the Development of Christian Doctrine*, Newman employs an arresting image to argue that the impossibility of isolating a living idea from "intercourse with the

---

[2] See Ian Ker, *Newman on Vatican II* (Oxford: Oxford University Press, 2014), 74–5.

world around" is not a threat to the integrity of a philosophical or religious idea, on the ground that "the stream is clearest near the spring," for "a philosophy or belief" becomes "more equable, and purer, and stronger, when its bed has become deep, and broad, and full. It necessarily rises out of an existing state of things, and for a time savours of the soil. Its vital element needs disengaging from what is foreign and temporary."[3]

A striking contemporary exemplification of this is the rise of the new ecclesial communities and movements, which realize in the concrete the ecclesiology of the Church as an organic community, which the Second Vatican Council, a Council almost entirely concerned with the Church, proposes in the first two chapters of *Lumen Gentium*, in which the Council defines the fundamental nature of the Church. They also exemplify Newman's point that Councils open up further developments because of what they do *not* say or stress, what they do not teach. For, apart from the Decrees on the Mission Activity of the Church *Ad Gentes* and on the Apostolate of the Laity *Apostolicam Actuositatem*, the Second Vatican Council was silent on the subject of evangelization, even in the Pastoral Constitution on the Church in the Modern World *Gaudium et Spes*—whereas these new religious movements are obviously of great importance for evangelization.

The rediscovery of the charismatic as opposed to hierarchical dimension of the Church was surely one of the great achievements of Vatican II, the first two chapters of *Lumen Gentium* explicitly referring to them no less than three times. Newman too was well aware of the importance of the charisms, both as an Anglican and as a Catholic, although he does not use the term which only came into use at Vatican II, St. Thomas Aquinas's phrase *gratia gratis data* having been previously used. His first written, as opposed to published, contribution to the Oxford Movement was a paper on the Church Fathers where he writes about how "a child's voice, as it is reported, was heard in the midst of the crowd to say, 'Ambrose is bishop,'" a prophetic voice since Ambrose at the time was only a catechumen awaiting baptism. In these sketches, Newman writes about how monasticism was a charism given to the Church at a time of great need. Newman himself was particularly attracted

---

[3] John Henry Newman, *An Essay on the Development of Christian Doctrine* (London: Longmans, Green & Co., 1909), 40.

by the charism of St. Philip Neri, whose Oratory he established in England. But, of course, he was well aware that the charism of St. Philip was far less important for the Church than the charisms of much greater figures like Ss Benedict, Dominic, and Ignatius Loyola. Indeed, he had intended to write a book about these charismatic giants, although, in the end, he only wrote the part about St. Benedict's monastic charism. Finally, of course, the Oxford or Tractarian Movement, which Newman initiated and led until his conversion to Rome, anticipated modern ecclesial movements, including as it did both clergy and laity.

One of the points Newman makes in his mini-theology of Councils is that Councils have unintended consequences. Thus, Vatican II's Dogmatic Constitution on Divine Revelation *Dei Verbum* wanted to stress that both revelation and faith are primarily of a personalist rather than propositional nature. If the pre-Vatican II understanding of faith and revelation was overly propositional, the pendulum now swung to the opposite extreme. But, for Newman, faith and revelation were both personalist and propositional. Similarly, Newman would not have been surprised that the Pastoral Constitution on the Church in the Modern World *Gaudium et Spes*, by far the longest of the documents of the Second Vatican Council, led to an undue emphasis on justice and peace as opposed to the central preaching of the Gospel. Moreover, the fact that the Constitution perfectly and correctly stressed the sovereignty of conscience but failed to add that the Catholic conscience is bound to attend carefully to the teachings of the Church predictably led to the idea that Catholics were free to dissent conscientiously from Church teachings. Or again, in the Constitution on the Sacred Liturgy *Sacrosanctum Concilium*, the emphasis on the liturgy as the source and summit of the Christian life led to the downgrading of popular devotions and, more seriously, of Eucharistic Adoration as well as the sacrament of Penance, which, it was thought, had been made redundant by the penitential rite at the beginning of Mass. Then again, the Declaration on the Relation of the Church to Non-Christian religions *Nostra Aetate*, which recognized the truth in these religions, led to the false idea that Christianity was just one of many authentic religions.

Newman's understanding of conscience has regularly been misunderstood. The famous toast in *Letter to the Duke of Norfolk*, "I shall drink—to the Pope, if you please—still to conscience first, and to the Pope afterwards,"[4] refers to orders not to teachings. Newman was responding to a pamphlet by the former prime minister, W. E. Gladstone, who had misinterpreted the definition of papal infallibility at the First Vatican Council as applying to papal edicts as well as teachings. But, in fact, the definition was entirely about definitions and is completely devoid of any reference to papal edicts, which, according to the tradition of the Church, should not be obeyed if immoral. Neither in the *Letter* nor anywhere else does Newman envisage the possibility of so-called conscientious dissent from Church teachings.

In contrast to the Second Vatican Council's relative silence about evangelization, in his second novel *Callista*, Newman addressed the problem of evangelizing a secularized as opposed to pagan world. For the heroine, Callista, is a post-pagan Greek girl, who in Greece had worshipped Apollo, but who now in North Africa "somehow" worships nothing, for, like Matthew Arnold with his "melancholy, long, withdrawing roar" of the "Sea of Faith,"[5] she is "weary," feeling "a weariness in all things."[6] Newman's well-known argument for the existence of God from the existence of conscience plays no role in her conversion. Rather, conversion to Christianity comes to her because it offers fulfillment and happiness. For Callista is

> a living, breathing woman with an over-flowing heart, with keen affections, with a yearning after some object which may possess me. I cannot exist without something to rest upon. I cannot fall back upon that drear, forlorn state, which philosophers call wisdom, and moralists call virtue … I must have something to love; love is my life.

But the Christian God, she is assured, "satisfies every affection of the heart."[7] For

> if you have needs, desires, aims, aspirations, all of which demand an Object, and imply, by their very existence, that such an Object does exist also, and if nothing here does satisfy them, and if

---

[4] John Henry Newman, *Certain Difficulties Felt by Anglicans in Catholic Teaching* (London: Longmans, Green & Co, 1900), II, 261.

[5] Matthew Arnold, "Dover Beach," in *New Poems* (London: Macmillan & Co., 1867), 112.

[6] John Henry Newman, *Callista: A Tale of the Third Century* (London: Longmans, Green & Co., 1901), 117.

[7] Ibid., 126, 130–3.

> there is a message which professes to come from that Object, of whom you already have the presentiment, and to teach you about Him, and to bring the remedy you crave; and if those who try that remedy say with one voice that the remedy answers; are you not bound at least, Callista, to look that way …?[8]

Callista demands to know what this "remedy" is, this "Object," this "love." And she is given by the priest Caecilius what Newman clearly thought was the best apologetic for the "new evangelization": that is, the evangelization of secular as opposed to pagan man—namely, a response to secular man's sense of unfulfillment and desire for happiness:

> Every man is in that state which you confess of yourself. We have no love for Him who alone lasts. We love those things which do not last, but come to an end. Things being thus, He whom we ought to love has determined to win us back to Him. With this object He has come into His own world, in the form of one of us men. And in that human form He opens His arms and woos us to return to Him, our Maker. This is our Worship, this is our Love, Callista.

And as time passed, the more Callista "thought over what she learned about Christianity, the more she was drawn to it, and the more it approved itself to her whole soul, and the more it seemed to respond to all her needs and aspirations."[9]

Callista is converted to the God of Christianity for the reason that Newman set out in one of his finest Anglican sermons "The Thought of God, the Stay of the Soul": namely, that, as he puts it in another sermon, "the Gospel … supplies our very need."[10] Without a personal God, Newman argues, a person "has faculties and affections without a ruling principle, object, or purpose." Arguing that "the happiness of the soul consists in the exercise of the affections," Newman contends that "here is at once a reason for saying that the thought of God, and nothing short of it, is the happiness of man," since "the affections require a something more vast and more enduring than anything created."[11] We recall St. Augustine's

---

[8] Ibid., 220–1.
[9] Ibid., 131–2.
[10] John Henry Newman, *Parochial and Plain Sermons* (London: Longmans, Green & Co., 1907), III, sermon 9, 124 (hereafter *PPS*).
[11] *PPS*, V, sermon 22, 314–16.

famous words, "our hearts are restless till they rest in you,"[12] when we read the equivalent in Newman: "He alone is sufficient for the hearts who made it." Other human beings cannot satisfy us, partly because they are transient and unreliable in their frailty: "our hearts require something more permanent and uniform than man can be ... Do not all men die? Are they not taken from us? Are they not as uncertain as the grass of the field?"

However, "there is another reason why God alone is the happiness of our souls," as Newman explains:

> The contemplation of Him, and nothing but it, is able fully to open and relieve the mind, to unlock, occupy, and fix our affections. We may indeed love things created with great intenseness, but such affection, when disjoined from the love of the Creator, is like a stream running in a narrow channel, impetuous, vehement, turbid. The heart runs out, as it were, only at one door; it is not an expanding of the whole man. Created natures cannot open us, or elicit the ten thousand mental senses which belong to us, and through which we really live. None but the presence of our Maker can enter us, for to none besides can the whole heart in all its thoughts and feelings be unlocked and subjected.

The love and sympathy of those closest to us cannot rival the intimacy we can enjoy with God alone:

> It is this feeling of simple and absolute confidence and communion, which soothes and satisfies those to whom it is vouchsafed. We know that even our dearest friends enter into us but partially, and hold intercourse with us only at times, whereas the consciousness of a perfect and enduring Presence, and it alone, keeps the heart open.

It is only ultimately God, then, who can liberate the human heart from the prison of the self:

> Withdraw the Object on which it rests, and it will relapse again into its state of confinement and constraint, and in proportion as it is limited either to certain seasons or to certain affections, the heart is straitened and distressed. If it be not over bold to say it, He who is infinite can alone be its measure. He alone can answer to that mysterious assemblage of feelings and thoughts which it has within it.

That is why true happiness depends on belief in God, as otherwise,

---

[12] St. Augustine, *Confessions*, I.1.

"We are pent up within ourselves and are therefore miserable."

> [We] need a relief to our hearts, that they may be dark and sullen no longer, or that they may not go on feeding upon ourselves; we need to escape from ourselves to something beyond; and much as we may wish it otherwise, and may try to make idols to ourselves, nothing short of God's presence is our true refuge; every thing else is either a mockery, or but an expedient useful for its season or in its measure.

And so it is not in the first place the voice of conscience that demands the existence of a personal God, but rather it is the self-seeking liberation from its self-imprisonment in the only object external to itself which can offer true personal fulfillment, for a person cannot properly "live without an object": either, then, we live in the unhappiness of the prison of our own self—or we try visibly to find self-fulfillment in other ephemeral people or things. As Newman put it in a particularly powerful passage, in the latter case, a person

> fancies that he is sufficient for himself; or he supposes that knowledge is sufficient for his happiness; or that exertion, or that the good opinion of others, or (what is called) fame, or that the comforts of luxury and wealth, are sufficient for him. What a truly wretched state is that coldness and dryness of soul, in which so many live and die. Many a great man, many a peasant, many a busy man, lives and dies with closed heart, with affections undeveloped and unexercised. You see the poor man, passing day after day, Sunday after Sunday, year after year, without a thought in his head, to appearance almost like a stone. You see the educated man, full of thought full of intelligence, full of action, but still with a stone heart, as cold and dead as regards his affections, as if he were the poor ignorant countryman. You see others, with warm affections, perhaps, for their families, with benevolent feelings towards their fellow-men. Yet stopping there, centring their hearts on what is sure to fail them, as being perishable. Life passes, riches fly away, popularity is fickle, the senses decay, the world changes, friends die. One alone is constant; One alone is true to us. One alone can be true to us; One alone can be true; One alone can be all things to us; One alone can supply our needs; One alone can train us up to our full perfection; One alone can give a meaning to our complex and intricate nature; One alone can form and possess us.[13]

---

[13] *PPS*, V, sermon 22, 316–19, 324–6.

"Heart Speaks to Heart"

In *Callista*, the apologetic of this great sermon is given dramatic actuality. Faced with the unbelief of secular man, Newman unabashedly appeals to our universal human desire for happiness and self-fulfillment, emphasizing not the dictates of conscience but the demands of self-interest, the need to respond to the "affections and aspirations pent up"[14] within the human heart.

---

[14] *PPS*, III, sermon 9, 124.

2

Homily for Mass at the Saint John Henry Newman Symposium

The Commemoration of All the Faithful Departed—
November 2, 2019
St. Joseph's Seminary, Dunwoodie, Yonkers, New York

Bishop John O. Barres, D.D., S.T.D.

As many of you may know, my parents converted to the Catholic faith. Oliver and Marjorie Barres, both graduates of the Yale Divinity School, both ordained Congregational ministers, were received into the Church on the Eve of Pentecost in 1955.

Layers of grace impact every conversion, and the conversions of my parents were no different. One layer of grace for them was the influence of now-Saint John Henry Cardinal Newman. His writings and heroic example aided my father and mother in their momentous decision to "set [their] face[s] absolutely towards the Wilderness," to borrow a phrase of Newman's, leave what was familiar, and enter the Catholic Church.[1]

This familial connection to Cardinal Newman made his canonization almost three weeks ago all the more exciting for me. For I know firsthand the evangelizing reach of this new saint, and, in this time of the New Evangelization and the need for dramatic

---

[1] The phrase is used by Newman in a letter to John Keble dated November 21, 1844, in Francis J. McGrath, ed., *The Letters and Diaries of John Henry Newman*, vol. X, *The Final Step: 1 November 1843 – 6 October 1845* (Oxford: Oxford University Press, 2006), 426..

"Heart Speaks to Heart"

missionary growth in the Church, it energizes me to contemplate St. John Henry Newman assisting us from on high. What St. John Henry Newman did for my parents and countless other converts, so I believe he can still do for those seeking the Truth today. His witness, his teachings, and his prayers before the throne of Mercy, can—and will—lead many to the one true fold of Christ or deepen their connection with it.

This firm conviction has motivated me in recent months to highlight St. John Henry Newman to the People of God of the Diocese of Rockville Centre. Through efforts on social media, on television through the Catholic Faith Network, and in a recent pastoral letter, we as a Diocese have striven to make Newman more widely known so that he may point us and others to the Kindly Light.

Our gathering these days in this venerable place of priestly and lay formation contributes to this diffusion of Cardinal Newman's life and thought, and it helps us approach Cardinal Newman to be our intercessor for a new Catholic springtime of evangelization in the state of New York, in the United States of America, and throughout our world.

Like you, I am grateful to the foresight of Msgr. Vaccari and his faculty who planned this symposium. The generosity of St. Joseph's Seminary in coordinating the event, assembling so many expert presenters, and opening its doors, allows us, so soon after the canonization, to let St. John Henry Newman's heart speak to our own. Thank you, Msgr. Vaccari.

TODAY'S PRESENTATIONS in the classrooms and our conversations in the hallways rightly focus on the saintly cardinal and his call to holiness. Yet, our prayer at Mass this morning, along with our prayer throughout this liturgical day, is caught up with something happening beyond the confines of Dunwoodie. For today, with the Church universal, we participate in a great spiritual work of mercy. As we do every year on November 2nd, we remember to the Father, Son, and Holy Spirit those who have gone before us. We commemorate all the faithful departed.

At this Holy Sacrifice of the Mass, we pray fervently that grace and mercy will be with all the holy souls, remembering especially in prayer those dear to us, our family members and friends, and as we see the many portraits of the Ordination classes here at Dunwoodie, we remember every one of those souls. We pray that God will find them worthy of himself and that they will pass over to a dwelling place of light and peace where they will shine.

Our wider secular society often thinks going forth from this world means utter destruction, that the dead are dead. Hence, society might think such prayer foolish. Better, in society's mind, simply to celebrate a life rather than partake in fancy. But our prayer for the dead is not wishful thinking, a sentimental balm. It does not stem from a fairy tale, but it is rooted in fact and truth. We pray confidently because of what God has done, because of his initiative, because of what he has accomplished in Christ.

Jesus Christ, the Lord who took our flesh, loved us to the end, dying for us while we were still yet sinners. His outstretched love, shown fully on the cross, unleashed a cosmic reconciliation with the Father, the reconciliation for which fallen humanity longed. This reconciliation won on the cross is fact and it produces hope which, as St. Paul reminds us, does not disappoint. Therefore, in hope, we pray at this Mass that those who have known the Son on their earthly pilgrimage will come to life eternal with him. We pray that they, the faithful departed, will hear those heartening words of our Alleluia verse: Come you blessed by my Father and inherit the kingdom prepared for you.

TODAY'S COMMEMORATION, and yesterday's Solemnity of All Saints with it, manifests a fundamental belief of our faith: the communion of the Church of heaven and earth.[2] In praying for the dead today, and in celebrating yesterday the festival of the heavenly Jerusalem, we pilgrims are brought again before the wondrous reality that transcends space and time: that is, our unity with those who have preceded us in the Mystical Body of Christ. We are reminded through living these feasts that, "We believe in the communion of all the faithful of Christ, those who are pilgrims on earth, the dead who are attaining their purification, and the blessed in heaven."[3]

Happily, these liturgical days stress communion, and it is this reality I wish to highlight in the life of St. John Henry Newman, especially the communion he lived in the pilgrim Church.

---

[2] Cf. *Catechism of the Catholic Church* (Citta del Vaticano: Libreria Editrice Vaticana, 1993), n. 954 & ff.
[3] Pope St. Paul VI, *Credo for the People of God*, June 30, 1968.

"Heart Speaks to Heart"

In a sermon from his Anglican days entitled "The Communion of Saints," Newman reminds us that those who belong to the Church must do more than speak about her, or contemplate her, or defend her. These things they may well do, and should do, but *love of the Church* must be at the heart of it all, at the heart of every thought, word or action. Love is key, and Newman proceeds to point out what loving the communion of the Church entails: loving the whole Church, the Church invisible and visible, the Church unseen and seen.

He makes special note of reminding his hearers to love what is *perceptible* to them when he says, "The test of our being joined to Christ is love; the test of love towards Christ and His Church is loving those whom we actually see." Newman goes on to say that if "we would be worthy to hold communion with believers of every time and place, let us hold communion duly with those of our own day and our own neighborhood."[4]

St. John Henry Cardinal Newman brings before us, in a beautifully gentle yet bold way, what we know, but perhaps in moments of weakness forget: namely, that loving the Church and living in communion with the Body of Christ means loving our neighbor.

When we are mindful of this Gospel imperative, or reminded of it by reading the Scriptures, examining our consciences, or through our spiritual reading, perhaps our impetus to love others turns towards helping those in material need. Such charity is important, it is a benchmark by which we will be judged, and Pope Francis constantly calls our attention towards the practice of such love. However, I would like to consider the spiritual dimension of loving our neighbor. For such spiritual love—that love which desires and acts for the best in a person's relationship with God—is no less a concrete way that strengthens the bonds of communion among the pilgrim Church.

Such spiritual, neighborly love was present in Newman's life and can instruct us in living our call to holiness. In his long sojourn, so full of examples, allow me to illustrate just one instance—that of Newman's reception into the Church—to showcase the power

---

[4] John Henry Newman, "The Communion of Saints," in *Parochial and Plain Sermons* (London: Longmans, Green & Co., 1909), IV, sermon 11, 184.

of one spiritually loving a neighbor. The story is familiar. In an intense moment, on October 9, 1845, Newman, having been deep in history and after years of prayer, was received into the Church at his beloved Littlemore on the outskirts of Oxford. The reception occurred at his desk by an iterant Italian Passionist priest, now-Blessed Dominic Barberi.

The scene caught in freezeframe captures Newman, not the cardinal or preacher or writer, but Newman the man seeking Christ more deeply on one side, and it reveals on the other Barberi as one attentive to the needs of a brother. In the scene, we might see many things, but let us focus on Newman as the recipient of Blessed Dominic's gentle, brotherly love: a love that drove the Passionist to be present there in Littlemore.

Being present was no easy feat. Barberi, you will recall, was Italian. He had arrived in England four years earlier at the age of 49. Even though he was older and without a great command of the English language, he felt impelled to preach Christ and make him known in England's cities and towns. It was a desire he had held in a quixotic way for most of his life.

What stirred him? What brought him to England? Perhaps, simply put, the spiritual well-being of his brothers and sisters. An attentiveness to the spiritual bonds of communion he held with those in a foreign land drove him to that mission territory, to be present in places like Littlemore, and it was the spiritual well-being of his friends in Christ that emboldened him to remain and endure great trials and hardships. The task was not easy, but his steadfastness and joy brought about conversions and, through Barberi, "a simple, holy man" as Newman relates in his *Apologia*, the mighty preacher of Oxford was received into the Church.

There was in Barberi more than a concern for Newman's spiritual well-being and the well-being of others, as beautiful as that was. There was holiness, too: personal holiness. In Newman's own words of tribute, Blessed Dominic was a "marvelous missioner and preacher filled with zeal." He was a priest with a powerful presence. Indeed, Newman observed that Blessed Dominic's "very look had about it something holy." Further, St. John Henry noted that, "When [the Passionist's] form came within sight, [he] was moved to the depths in the strangest way." Thus, we might say, the keys to Barberi's missionary fruitfulness are laid bare: first, an attentiveness to the obligations of communion, that is, to love; and, second, personal holiness.

In the Church's life, holiness begets holiness. It happens down the centuries, and I am fascinated by the Spirit's work. Saints fuel other saints. Not surprisingly, then, the holy life of Blessed Dominic was transmitted, so to speak, to Newman, brief as their interaction was, and served as an inspiration. Thus, like Barberi, Newman, while striving for personal holiness to fulfill his mission in this life, employed, among the many tools at his disposal and in his own way, a deep love for the spiritual good of those around him. His motto, *Heart Speaks to Heart*, sums up well that mission. Through these means—holiness and attentiveness—he, too, became a fruitful missionary in his own land, personally influencing a great number of converts, and inspiring from afar many more, including Oliver and Marjorie Barres.

The bond of communion that united Blessed Dominic Barberi and St. John Henry Newman during their earthly pilgrimages exists between us. We have communion with them, yes, and we, who currently see through the glass dimly in our walk toward the Lord, have communion with each other. It is our duty to live and strengthen the bond between us.

May Blessed Dominic and St. John Henry teach us. May they instruct us to love those around us by being attentive to their spiritual welfare. Further, may they encourage us to influence others by fearlessly pursuing our own radical call to holiness.

May we be docile to receive others into our life, and may we be bold in giving a witness of holiness. St. John Henry Newman and Blessed Dominic Barberi did so, and explosive growth followed. May we do our part, may we live in communion and strive for sanctity, and may dramatic missionary growth, the Lord's doing, follow.

Blessed Dominic Barberi, pray for us!
St. John Henry Cardinal Newman, pray for us!

3

Saint John Henry Cardinal Newman and the Standard of Saintliness

Edward Short

He who would fully and feelingly undertake the work of Christ must study to make his whole life conformable to that of Christ.
     Thomas à Kempis, *The Imitation of Christ* (1418–27)

TO SPEAK OF THE SAINT in St. John Henry Newman is to speak of a man who gave his entire adult life not only to embodying heroic virtue himself but guiding others to embody it as well. Proof of the efficacy of his personal influence in this line abounds in his letters. "I cannot help thinking of you always on the Epiphany," James Stewart, Professor of Greek and Latin in the Catholic University of Ireland, wrote the great convert in January of 1870, "for it was on that day I and my family were received into the Church, twenty years ago, and we never can forget how entirely it was owing to you that humanly speaking we ever became Catholics":

> Your sermons as a Protestant broke up the hardened protestant soil of my heart, and your sermons to mixed congregations was the last book I read before I became a Catholic; and my doubts and difficulties about the Blessed Virgin were dispelled by your two sermons in that volume, especially the one on "The Glories of Mary for the sake of her Son." You will never know how many people owe their conversion to you ... till the day when all hearts are open."[1]

---

[1] James Stewart to John Henry Newman (January 6, 1870), in Charles Stephen Dessain *et al.*, eds., *The Letters and Diaries of John Henry Newman*, vols. I–XXXII (Oxford and London: Thomas Nelson, 1961–2008; hereafter *LD*), XXV, 7. Stewart converted in 1849. There is a biographical entry on him in *LD*,

"Heart Speaks to Heart"

This testimonial also confirms how much Newman's life exemplifies the practical wisdom of the Catechism, which has this to say of the relationship between holiness and canonization:

> By canonizing some of the faithful, i.e., by solemnly proclaiming that they practiced heroic virtue and lived in fidelity to God's grace, the Church recognizes the power of the Spirit of holiness within her and sustains the hope of believers by proposing the saints to them as models and intercessors. "The saints have always been the source and origin of renewal in the most difficult moments in the Church's history." Indeed, "holiness is the hidden source and infallible measure of her apostolic activity and missionary zeal."[2]

Now that Newman has been canonized, we can see how much his life reaffirms the holiness essential to the Church's "apostolic activity and missionary zeal." Nowhere else is this more radiantly clear than in his sermon entitled "The Spiritual Mind" (1831), in which he proclaims:

> We must have a deep sense of our guilt, and of the difficulty of securing heaven; we must live as in His presence, daily pleading His cross and passion, thinking of His holy commandments, imitating His sinless pattern, and depending on the gracious aids of His Spirit; that we may really and truly be servants of Father, Son, and Holy Ghost, in whose name we were baptized. Further, we must, for His sake, aim at a noble and unusual strictness of life, perfecting holiness in His fear, destroying our sins, mastering our whole soul, and bringing it into captivity to His law, denying ourselves lawful things, in order to do Him service, exercising a profound humility, and an unbounded, never-failing love, giving away much of our substance in religious and charitable works, and discountenancing and shunning irreligious men. This is to be a Christian; a gift easily described, and in a few words, but attainable only with fear and much trembling.[3]

---

according to which, "In 1853 Newman tried to obtain his services for the boys living in the Oratory, but in Aug. he went as tutor to the sons of R. J. Gainford, at Darnall Hall, Sheffield. Later in the year he agreed to be one of Newman's four tutors at Dublin. In October 1854, Newman appointed Stewart Lecturer in Ancient History at the Catholic University. He was Professor of the Greek and Latin languages 1857–91, and in 1880 became one of the first Fellows of the Royal University of Ireland." *LD*, XXII, 373.

[2] "The Church is Holy" (828), *Catechism of the Catholic Church* (New York: Doubleday: 1995), 238–9.

[3] John Henry Newman, *Parochial and Plain Sermons* (London: Longmans, Green

This is hardly the sort of thing that we are used to hearing from many of our current Catholic pulpits; but, then, the fact that we hear it now from Newman the saint—when not only our social order but the Roman Church is in such a parlous way—is surely providential. *Pace* the Modernists in our midst, Newman never suggests that it might be pleasing to God that we forsake the devout life. The very fact that he insists on that devout life is what makes him so salutary for us. What is it that G. K. Chesterton said in his *St. Thomas Aquinas* (1933)? "It is the paradox of history that each generation is converted by the saint who contradicts it most ... In a world that was too stolid, Christianity returned in the form of a vagabond; in a world that has grown a great deal too wild, Christianity has returned in the form of a teacher of logic."[4] Speaking here of St. Francis and St. Thomas, Chesterton could not have known that our own world would be blessed with an even more countercultural saint. Yet so it is. In St. John Henry Cardinal Newman, we have been given the saint we need most.

Before delving into Newman's dedication to holiness, I should say something of his life. Born in London in 1801, he was the son of John Newman, a Lombard Street banker, the son, in turn, of a Mayfair grocer, originally from Cambridgeshire, and Jemima (*née*) Fourdrinier, the daughter of a printer of Norman Huguenot stock, whose family became famous for their paper making and, indeed, their paper-making machines. Newman was the eldest of six children, with two younger brothers and three sisters, none of whom understood his embrace of a Roman Catholic faith synonymous in nineteenth-century England with treachery, backwardness, superstition and irrationality. The one exception might have been his beloved sister Mary, who died suddenly at the age of nineteen in 1828.[5] Indeed, it was her death that inspired one of Newman's

---

    & Co., 1907), I, sermon 6, 80 (hereafter *PPS*).

[4] Gilbert Keith Chesterton, *Saint Thomas Aquinas—"The Dumb Ox"* (New York: Sheed & Ward, 1933), 8–9.

[5] Newman's account of Mary shortly after her death shows that he saw exceptional sanctity in his beloved sister. "To us all her sudden death is of course a most bitter affliction—yet it is graciously softened by numberless merciful alleviations, and we one and all feel from our hearts (and have from the very first felt) a strong conviction that it is most good and right and desirable—and we bless God for it—all our recollections connected with dear Mary are sweet—and our sorrow at her loss is borne down by the remembrance of what she was to us, our joy and delight,—and the hope

most powerful sermons, "The Invisible World" (1837), in which he told his incredulous contemporaries: "The world of spirits … though unseen, is present; present, not future, not distant. It is not above the sky, it is not beyond the grave; it is now and here; the kingdom of God is among us."[6] Of course, as Our Lord found to his chagrin, no prophet is loved in his own country,[7] and this was certainly true in Newman's case. However, he mitigated this, first, by winning his contemporaries' admiration in his controversy with Charles Kingsley, which culminated in his *Apologia pro Vita Sua* (1865) and by being made a cardinal by Pope Leo XIII in 1879. Since Newman was born under the shadow of the French Revolution and lived to see the arrival of what he called in his *Biglietto* Speech the "great *Apostasia*," he lived in a time ripe not only for conversion but reconversion. As both an Anglican in Oxford and a Catholic in Birmingham—he was received into the Church of Rome in 1845—as a priest, poet, theologian, historian, philosopher, novelist, and educator, he worked sedulously to impress upon his contemporaries the reality of God's love. This is why he was preoccupied with holiness, with purity, with living in accordance with God's commandments. This is also why 20,000 people lined the funeral procession of his cortège after he died in Birmingham on the 11th of August in 1890.[8]

---

of what she will be when we meet her before the throne of God. Few of course can know what she was—we know her mind to have been rare indeed and intensely beautiful. She was gifted with that singular sweetness and affectionateness of temper that she lived in an ideal world of happiness, the very sight of which made others happy. All that happened to her she could change into something bright and smiling like herself—all events, all persons (almost) she loved and delighted in—and thus, having lived in this world as if it were heaven, before she discovered (as she must in time) that it was not so, she has been translated into the real and substantial heaven of God. For myself indeed, I have for years been so affected with her unclouded cheerfulness and extreme guilelessness of heart that I have be[come] impressed with the conviction that she would not live long, and have almost anticipated her death." John Henry Newman to Robert Isaac Wilberforce (January 14, 1828), in *LD*, II, 49–50.

[6] *PPS*, IV, sermon 13, 207.
[7] See Lk 4:24.
[8] For a study of Newman's relationship to his parents and siblings, see Edward Short, *Newman and his Family* (London: Bloomsbury, 2013). For a detailed account of Newman's funeral, see *LD*, XXXII, 647–60. In the same volume, the editor Francis J. McGrath, FMS, includes all the contemporary obituaries published after Newman's death. See pp. 537–688.

Newman and the Standard of Saintliness

Now for his life of sanctity, the life of the saint ... Newman once said that his true *métier* was education,[9] which was true enough, though it is vital to appreciate that the education Newman had in mind was the education necessary for men to lead lives of sanctity, since it was only by leading such lives that they could enter into the glory of God's love for them and be the men that God intended them to be.[10] The provost of Oriel College, Edward Hawkins, no sooner got wind of Newman's pastoral view of education than he barred him from tutoring, claiming, not altogether ingenuously, that it led to favoritism. In all events, then, as now, taking a pastoral view of the tutorial charge was not an acceptable view. The Oxford don Mark Pattison, certainly no biased observer of these proceedings, held that: "This year, 1831,"—the year after Hawkins forbade Newman from tutoring—"was the turning point in the fortunes of Oriel. From this date the College began to go downhill, both in the calibre of the men who obtained Fellowships and in the style and tone of the undergraduates."[11] It is also from this date that a certain administrative stultification began to afflict Oxford, a stultification about which Pattison, with his contempt for the busy work of bureaucracies, was marvelously acid, likening the tone of college administrators to that of "a lively municipal borough; all the objects of science and learning, for which a university exists, being put out of sight by the consideration of the material means

---

[9] "Now, from first to last, education, in the large sense of the word, has been my line," *John Henry Newman: Autobiographical Writings*, ed. Henry Tristram (New York: Sheed & Ward, 1955), 259. While acknowledging that his interest in Catholic education put "conversions comparatively in the background," Newman was also adamant that the education of Catholics was vital if conversions to the Faith were to be well-grounded and lasting. On this score, the cautionary tale of the fickle Reverend Richard Waldo Sibthorp (1792–1879) was never far from his mind.

[10] See Paul Shrimpton, *The "Making of Men": The Idea and Reality of Newman's University in Oxford and Dublin* (Leominster: Gracewing, 2014), 468–70.

[11] Mark Pattison, *Memoirs* (London: Macmillan, 1885), 88. According to James Anthony Froude's biographer, Ciaran Brady, "the decline was rather less gentle" than Pattison suggested. "In the early 1820s Oriel was responsible for 15 percent of all First Class degrees awarded by the university, by the later 1830s it was gaining less than 5 percent, and by the close of the 1840s, in the carefully calibrated league table constructed by Sir William Hamilton, Oriel was placed decisively in the second division of Oxford's twenty-four colleges." Ciaran Brady, *James Anthony Froude: An Intellectual Biography of a Victorian Prophet* (Oxford: Oxford University Press, 2013), 72.

of endowing them."[12] For Newman, in contrast, preparing those under his tutelage to enter into the stakes inherent in the truth of God's promises would remain the essence of the educational charge. And he did this, pre-eminently, by personifying the Christian belief that he wished those under his charge to discover for themselves.[13] That this should have been confirmed most memorably by the Whig historian and acolyte of Carlyle, Anthony James Froude may be an odd irony; but Froude, like Pattison, despite his religious differences with Newman, never left off admiring him.[14] "It has been said that men of letters are either much less or much greater than their writings," Froude wrote in a brilliant essay on Newman's influence in Oxford that he included in his *Short Studies on Great Subjects* (1883):

> Greatly as his poetry had struck me, he was himself all that the poetry was, and something far beyond. I had then never seen so impressive a person. I met him now and then in private; I attended his church and heard him preach Sunday after Sunday; he is supposed to have been insidious, to have led his disciples

---

[12] Pattison, *Memoirs*, 90.

[13] See John Henry Newman, "Personal Influence, The Means of Propagating the Truth" (1832), in *Fifteen Sermons Preached in the University of Oxford*, ed. James David Earnest and Gerard Tracey (Oxford: Oxford University Press, 2006), 62–77.

[14] While an Oriel undergraduate, Froude only worked closely with Newman briefly in the Spring of 1843 on *The Lives of the English Saints*; but, as his biographer attests, he left a deep impression on the older brother of Newman's great friend, Hurrell Froude. The elder Froude, "like so many others, found it impossible not to admire Newman from afar. In part this was due to Newman's ... donnish charisma. Froude recalled Newman not as an austere or grave ascetic, but as a kind, gentle and witty man who moved easily among the undergraduates at Oriel, impressing them with his reputation as a connoisseur of wine, his ... knowledge of recent military history, and conversing informally with them on the 'subjects of the day, of literature, of public persons and incidents, of everything which was generally interesting.' No wonder the Oriel undergraduates, Froude says, proudly declaimed *Credo in Newmannum*." Brady, *James Anthony Froude*, 87–8. The other reason why Froude was drawn to and admired Newman is that he saw in him something of his own critical detachment from the views of others, though Froude's own views on the English Reformation, Ireland, and Carlyle, not to mention the West Indies were always more *outré* than judicious. As for Pattison, until the end of his days, he kept a framed photograph of Newman on his study's mantlepiece. See H. S Jones, *Intellect and Character in Victorian England: Mark Pattison and the Invention of the Don* (Cambridge: Cambridge University Press, 2007), 9.

on to conclusions to which he designed to bring them, while his purpose was carefully veiled. He was, on the contrary, the most transparent of men. He told us what he believed to be true. He did not know where it would carry him. No one who has ever risen to any great height in this world refuses to move till he knows where he is going. He is impelled in each step which he takes by a force within himself. He satisfies himself only that the step is a right one, and he leaves the rest to Providence. Newman's mind was world-wide. He was interested in everything which was going on in science, in politics, in literature. Nothing was too large for him, nothing too trivial, if it threw light upon the central question, what man really was, and what was his destiny.[15]

Newman's "venture of faith," as he called it, has never been so elegantly epitomized,[16] nor his appreciation of the stakes of faith, even for the agnostic Froude:

Where Christianity is a real belief, where there are distinct convictions that a man's own self and the millions of human beings who are playing on the earth's surface are the objects of a supernatural dispensation, and are on the road to heaven or hell, the most powerful mind may well be startled at the aspect of things. If Christianity was true, since Christianity was true (for Newman at no time doubted the reality of the revelation), then modern England, modern Europe, with its march of intellect and its useful knowledge and its material progress, was advancing with a light heart into ominous conditions.[17]

That we are now confronted by "ominous conditions" of our own, thanks to our uncritical trust in the intellect, makes Froude's insights into Newman's wariness of the intellect all the more compelling.

Moreover, Newman, who is always admirably practical about the life of grace, richly corroborates what Froude has to say here by speaking of how the sense of the supernatural gradually emerges in the otherwise distracted mind in a way that pointedly appeals to each one of us. We can see this in his sermon "The Immortality of the Soul" (1833): "To understand that we have souls is to feel our separation from things visible, our independence of them, our distinct existence in ourselves, our individuality, our power

---

[15] James Anthony Froude, "The Oxford Counter-Reformation," in *Short Studies on Great Subjects* (London: Longmans & Green, 1883), 196.
[16] See John Henry Newman, "The Ventures of Faith" (1836), *PPS*, IV, sermon 20.
[17] Froude, "The Oxford Counter-Reformation," 197.

of acting for ourselves this way or that way, our accountableness for what we do," Newman says.

> These are the great truths which lie wrapped up indeed even in a child's mind, and which God's grace can unfold there in spite of the influence of the external world; but at first this outward world prevails. We look off from self to the things around us, and forget ourselves in them. Such is our state,—a depending for support on the reeds which are no stay, and overlooking our real strength,—at the time when God begins His process of reclaiming us to a truer view of our place in His great system of providence. And when He visits us, then in a little while there is a stirring within us. The unprofitableness and feebleness of the things of this world are forced upon our minds; they promise but cannot perform, they disappoint us. Or, if they do perform what they promise, still (so it is) they do not satisfy us. We still crave for something, we do not well know what; but we are sure it is something which the world has not given us. And then its changes are so many, so sudden, so silent, so continual. It never leaves changing; it goes on to change, till we are quite sick at heart:—then it is that our reliance on it is broken. It is plain we cannot continue to depend upon it, unless we keep pace with it, and go on changing too; but this we cannot do. We feel that, while it changes, we are one and the same; and thus, under God's blessing, we come to have some glimpse of the meaning of our independence of things temporal, and our immortality.[18]

For Newman, it is only when this recognition of our immortality arrests our otherwise restless nature that we can begin to understand what that something is for which we crave. Moreover, in a sermon entitled "The Thought of God, The Stay of The Soul" (1839), he insists that this process of recognition takes place in our affections, which, when one thinks of it, is a rather beautiful way of treating the matter, for we all know that when our affections are truly stirred, rightly stirred, deeply stirred, we are at our best. And in Newman's testament to this truth, we can see the real *caritas* he felt for others:

> I say, then, that the happiness of the soul consists in the exercise of the affections; not in sensual pleasures, not in activity, not in excitement, not in self-esteem, not in the consciousness of power, not in knowledge; in none of these things lies our happiness, but

---

[18] PPS, I, sermon 2, 20.

in our affections being elicited, employed, supplied. As hunger and thirst, as taste, sound, and smell, are the channels through which this bodily frame receives pleasure, so the affections are the instruments by which the soul has pleasure. When they are exercised duly, it is happy; when they are undeveloped, restrained, or thwarted, it is not happy. This is our real and true bliss, not to know, or to affect, or to pursue; but to love, to hope, to joy, to admire, to revere, to adore. Our real and true bliss lies in the possession of those objects on which our hearts may rest and be satisfied. Now, if this be so, here is at once a reason for saying that the thought of God, and nothing short of it, is the happiness of man; for though there is much besides to serve as subject of knowledge, or motive for action, or means of excitement, yet the affections require a something more vast and more enduring than anything created. What is novel and sudden excites, but does not influence; what is pleasurable or useful raises no awe; self moves no reverence, and mere knowledge kindles no love. He alone is sufficient for the heart who made it.[19]

When we read such writing—writing which seems as though it had been written for each one of us alone, so accurate is the measure it takes of our own intimate longing for God—we might be lulled into imagining that knowing, loving and serving God is an easy business. Newman, however, rarely lets us forget that, for fallen human nature, rebellious, proud, intractable human nature, sanctity is never an easy business.[20] And one way he does this is by sharing with us the fate of the man who either rejects or despairs of following the counsels of sanctity. In reading of this hapless soul, we soon discover that Newman is not speaking of any imaginary creature. "He is at present attempting to satisfy his soul with that which is not bread," Newman writes,

> or he thinks the soul can thrive without nourishment. He fancies he can live without an object. He fancies that he is sufficient for himself; or he supposes that knowledge is sufficient for his happiness; or that exertion, or that the good opinion of others,

---

[19] *PPS*, V, sermon 22, 316. Newman's last sentence here nicely echoes St. Augustine's *Confessions* (I, 1): "Thou hast made us for Thyself, and the heart of man is restless until it finds its rest in Thee."

[20] One notable exception to this is Newman's "A Short Road to Perfection" (September 27, 1856), which can be found in John Henry Newman, *Prayers, Verses and Devotions*, introduced by Louis Bouyer (San Francisco: Ignatius Press, 1989), 328–9.

> or (what is called) fame, or that the comforts and luxuries of wealth, are sufficient for him. What a truly wretched state is that coldness and dryness of soul, in which so many live and die, high and low, learned and unlearned. Many a great man, many a peasant, many a busy man, lives and dies with closed heart, with affections undeveloped, unexercised. You see the poor man, passing day after day, Sunday after Sunday, year after year, without a thought in his mind, to appearance almost like a stone. You see the educated man, full of thought, fall of intelligence, full of action, but still with a stone heart, as cold and dead as regards his affections, as if he were the poor ignorant countryman. You see others, with warm affections, perhaps, for their families, with benevolent feelings towards their fellow-men, yet stopping there; centering their hearts on what is sure to fail them, as being perishable.[21]

No honest reader can read that passage without seeing something of himself in its unsparing assessment of human hard-heartedness. Moreover, Newman gives his cautionary sermon added urgency by reminding his reader that throughout this progress of blithe self-complacency, the clock is ticking. "Life passes, riches fly away, popularity is fickle, the senses decay, the world changes, friends die."[22] In the *Apologia*, Newman boldly declares that God sent his infallible Church into the world to restrain "the all-corroding, all-dissolving scepticism of the intellect ... to rescue it from its own suicidal excesses."[23] Yet, here he also acknowledges that God has sent his infallible Church into the world to meet the needs of the heart, for "One alone is constant; One alone is true to us; One alone can be true; One alone can be all things to us; One alone can supply our needs; One alone can train us up to our full perfection; One alone can give a meaning to our complex and intricate nature; One alone can give us tune and harmony; One alone can form and possess us."[24]

Again, in this moving passage, one can hear Newman's solicitude for his readers. He does not write to confirm them in their worldly impulses: he writes to show them the way to the unworldly sanctity without which they cannot know, love and serve God. By the

---

[21] *PPS*, V, sermon 22, 325–6.
[22] Ibid., 326.
[23] John Henry Newman, *Apologia pro Vita Sua*, ed. M. J. Svaglic (Oxford: Oxford University Press, 1967), 218.
[24] *PPS*, V, sermon 22, 326.

same token, Newman is always intent on encouraging those who might yearn to live the devout life but find themselves enmeshed in the world's toils. In his sermon "Saintliness Not Forfeited by the Penitent" (1842), he asks,

> Is it possible to conceive a greater contrast than is placed before us in the picture of Saul the persecutor of the Church, and of St. Paul, Apostle, Confessor, and Martyr? Who so great an enemy of Christ? who so true a servant? Nor is St. Paul's instance solitary; stranger cases still have occurred in the times after him. Not unregenerate sinners only like him, but those who have sinned after their regeneration; not sinners in ignorance only, like him, but those who knew what was right and did it not; not merely the blinded by a false zeal and an unhumbled heart, like him, but sensual, carnal, abandoned persons; profligates, who sacrificed to Satan body as well as soul; these, too, by the wonder-working grace of God, have from time to time become all that they were not; as high in the kingdom of heaven as they were before low plunged in darkness and in the shadow of death. Such awful instances of Christ's power meet us every now and then in the course of the Church's history.[25]

For Newman, such insignia of grace have a welcome moral. "They prove … that no degree of sin, however extreme … precludes the acquisition of any degree of holiness, however high. No sinner so great, but he may, through God's grace, become a saint ever so great."[26] At the same time, when he was in Milan in 1846, he likened learning sanctity to learning a foreign language. "How bad our pronunciation must be to the angels," he jotted down in his diary, "and in learning a language one is better one day, worse another."[27] But in insisting on the practicability of sanctity, Newman also reminds his readers of a perennial pitfall. "Men of this world, carnal men, unbelieving men, do not believe that the temptations which they themselves experience and to which they yield, can be overcome," he writes in his sermon "Saintliness the Standard of Christian Principle" (1849).

> They reason themselves into the notion that to sin is their very nature, and, therefore, is no fault of theirs; that is, they deny the

---

[25] John Henry Newman, *Sermons Bearing on Subjects of the Day* (London: J. G. F. and J. Rivington, 1869), 2–16.
[26] Ibid., 17.
[27] Diary entry for October 22, 1846, *LD*, XI, 264.

existence of sin.[28] And accordingly, when they read about the Saints or about holy men generally, they conclude either that these have not had the temptations which they experienced themselves, or that they have not overcome them. They either consider such an one to be a hypocrite, who practises in private the sins which he denounces that he never felt the temptation, and they regard him as a cold and simple person, who has never outgrown his childhood, who has a contracted mind, who does not know the world and life, who is despicable while he is without influence, and dangerous and detestable from his very ignorance when he is in power. But no, my brethren; read the lives of the Saints, you will see how false and narrow a view this is; these men, who think, forsooth, they know the world so well, and the nature of man so deeply, they know nothing of one great far-spreading phenomenon in man,—and that is, his nature under the operation of grace; they know nothing of the second nature, of the supernatural gift, induced by the Almighty Spirit upon our first and fallen nature; they have never met, they have never read of, and they have formed no conception of, a Saint.[29]

Newman himself gives an excellent illustration of this when, in his sermon "Men, Not Angels, the Priests of the Gospel" (1849), he speaks of the apostle of the apostles:

the blessed Magdalen, who had lived a life of shame; so much so, that even to be touched by her was, according to the religious judgment of her day, a pollution. Happy in this world's goods, young and passionate, she had given her heart to the creature, before the grace of God prevailed with her. Then she cut off her long hair, and put aside her gay apparel, and became so utterly what she had not been, that, had you known her before and after, you had said it was two persons you had seen, not one; for there was no trace of the sinner in the penitent, except the affectionate heart, now set on heaven and Christ; no trace besides, no memory of that glittering and seductive apparition,

---

[28] In his great purgatorial poem, "The Dream of Gerontius" (1865), which Edward Elgar set to such an enrapturing music, Newman makes no bones about the contempt for sanctity that obtains in those who deny the reality of sin. "What's a saint," he has his Demons ask. "One whose breath / Doth the air taint / Before his death / A bundle of bones / Which fools adore / Ha! ha!" John Henry Newman, *Verses on Various Occasions* (London: Longmans, Green, and Co., 1867), 345.

[29] John Henry Newman, *Discourses Addressed to Mixed Congregations* (London: Longman, Brown, Green & Longman, 1849), 97–8.

> in the modest form, the serene countenance, the composed gait, and the gentle voice of her who in the garden sought and found her Risen Saviour."[30]

If St. Mary Magdalen's sanctity is emblematic of love, the sanctity of St. Philip Neri and St. Ignatius Loyola is emblematic of humility. In his early Catholic sermon "Surrender to God" (1848), Newman writes of this with memorable historical insight. St. Philip and St. Ignatius, he says,

> were both great masters in their own persons of the grace of abstinence and fasting. Their own personal asceticism was wonderful, and yet these two great lights, though so different from each other, and so mortified themselves, agreed in this— not to impose bodily afflictions to any great extent on their disciples, but mortification of the spirit, of the will, of the affections, of the tastes, of the judgement, of the reason. They were divinely enlightened to see that the coming age, at the beginning of which they stood, required more than anything else, not mortification of the body (though it needed that too, of course,) but ... mortification of the reason and the will.[31]

Indeed, for Newman, this readiness on the part of both saints to rein in what he called "the wild living intellect of man"[32] was an exemplification of St. Philip's great maxim that "'a man's sanctity rests within the compass of three inches,' that is to say, in the due management of his brain."[33] In our own age, in which the academy calls for the transgressing of gender, the travestying of marriage, and the butchering of babies, among so many other ideological irrationalities, we can see the monstrosities that follow from the unshriven intellect.

If we turn to the very first sermon of Newman's *Parochial and Plain Sermons*, sermons which cover the entirety of his Anglican ministry from the 1820s to the 1840s and prefigure all of his Catholic work, we can see that its very title captures the essence of his preoc-

---

[30] Ibid., 3, 52. For an excellent and altogether Newmanian piece of hagiography, which I am grateful to my dear friend Margaret Fernandez for pointing out to me, see Father Sean Davidson, *Saint Mary Magdalene: Prophetess of Eucharistic Love* (San Francisco: Ignatius, 2017).

[31] John Henry Newman, *Faith and Prejudice and Other Unpublished Sermons of Cardinal Newman* (New York: Sheed & Ward, 1956), 70.

[32] *Apologia pro Vita Sua*, 219.

[33] St. Philip Neri, cited in John Henry Newman to Ambrose St. John (November 9, 1855), in *LD*, XVII, 48.

cupation with the devout life, entitled as it is "Holiness Necessary for Future Blessedness" (1826). Being the good Aristotelian that he was, Newman begins the sermon by defining what he means by "holiness." For Newman, "To be holy is ... to be separate from sin, to hate the works of the world, the flesh, and the devil; to take pleasure in keeping God's commandments; to do things as He would have us do them; to live habitually as in the sight of the world to come, as if we had broken the ties of this life, and were dead already."[34]

These, to men of the world, might seem unduly harsh criteria. Are we really called to "hate the works of the world?" Baron von Hügel, the friend and confidante of the Modernist George Tyrrell, used to say that Newman's Anglican sermons were too dour. Indeed, he once wrote his niece: "As a point of detail I had thought of starting you on Newman's *Parochial and Plain Sermons*," which he considered "certainly classics and well known to me." But he thought them, as he said, too "rigorist" ... Just the opposite from Fenélon, who always braces me. And really, I cannot allow you to be depressed."[35] For von Hügel, such "rigorism" was unchristian. "I hate rigorism, it's all wrong," he wrote. "Our Lord was never a rigorist. He loved publicans and sinners."[36] This is strikingly similar to what we hear from the antinomians in the hierarchy forever clamoring for their "paradigm shift."[37] We cannot insist

---

[34] *PPS*, I, sermon 1, 2–3.
[35] *Baron Friedrich von Hügel's Letters to a Niece*, ed. Gwendolen Greene (London and Toronto: J. M. Dent & Sons, 1928), 114–15. I am indebted to Father Robert Imbelli for pointing out these letters to me over dinner at that splendid Manhattan oasis, Antonucci's Cafe.
[36] *Ibid.*, xxiii.
[37] Cf., "In *Stimmen der Zeit* (November 2016), Cardinal Kasper insisted that Pope Francis' *Amoris Laetitia*, 'speaks not from an abstract image of the family thought out at a desk, but a realistic one of the joys as well as the difficulties in family life today ... it addresses sexuality and eroticism openly and in a relaxed manner expressing understanding and appreciation for the good that can also be found in situations that are not or not fully conforming to church teaching and ordinance.' Here, Cardinal Kasper had moved a world away from the ancient tradition that he had once praised Newman for reaffirming. Yet he expressly invoked Newman to justify these grave deviations, claiming that the Church's teaching on marriage

> does not change but it can be made more profound, it can be different. There is also a certain growth in the understanding of the Gospel and the doctrine, a development. Our famous Cardinal Newman had spoken on the development of doctrine. This is also not a change but

too finely on holiness or sanctity because we do not wish to be thought "rigid."

Yet, the saint in Newman had a decidedly different view of the matter. In his sermon, he concedes that God's insisting on holiness might seem, on the face of it, too demanding. Reflecting on the text "Holiness, without which no man shall see the Lord" (Heb 12:14), he says, in his best barristerial way:

> Now someone may ask, "Why is it that holiness is a necessary qualification for our being received into heaven? why is it that the Bible enjoins upon us so strictly to love, fear, and obey God, to be just, honest, meek, pure in heart, forgiving, heavenly-minded, self-denying, humble, and resigned? Man is confessedly weak and corrupt; why then is he enjoined to be so religious, so unearthly? *why* is he required (in the strong language of Scripture) to become 'a new creature'? Since he is by nature what he is, would it not be an act of greater mercy in God to save him altogether without this holiness, which it is so difficult, yet (as it appears) so necessary for him to possess?"[38]

The answer Newman gives to the suppositious critic of holiness—the critic of what might seem the unwarrantable "rigidity" of holiness, if you will—cannot be more salutary in the antinomian shambles in which the Church currently finds herself. "I answer as follows," he says, "that, even supposing a man of unholy life were suffered to enter heaven, *he would not be happy there*; so that it would be no mercy to permit him to enter."[39] In thus extolling the devout life so uncompromisingly, Newman was harkening back to the very thing that had made Christianity so attractive to the first-century Mediterranean, mired as it was in despondent hedonism. Chesterton memorably makes this point in his book *Heretics* (1905): "The great psychological discovery of

> > a development on the same line. Of course, the pope wants it and the world needs it. We live in a globalized world and you cannot govern everything from the Curia. There must be a common faith, a common discipline but a different application.
>
> This is the celebrated 'paradigm shift,' as he called it, borrowing a phrase from Thomas Kuhn, the philosopher of science ... Reading this, one can see that Cardinal Kasper's ideas of development ... have nothing to do with the authentic development reaffirmed by Newman." Edward Short, "Beware the Kasperization of Newman," *The Catholic Thing* (August 31, 2019).

[38] *PPS*, I, sermon 1, 1–2.
[39] Ibid., 3.

Paganism, which turned it into Christianity can be expressed with some accuracy in one phrase," he says. "The pagan set out, with admirable sense, to enjoy himself. By the end of his civilization he had discovered that a man cannot enjoy himself and continue to enjoy anything else."[40] Now, if there are any *roués* in the house this evening, any conscience-stricken *bon vivants*, let them ponder that! For Newman,

> A careless, a sensual, an unbelieving mind, a mind destitute of the love and fear of God, with narrow views and earthly aims, a low standard of duty, and a benighted conscience, a mind contented with itself, and unresigned to God's will, would feel as little pleasure, at the last day, at the words, "Enter into the joy of thy Lord," as it does now at the words, "Let us pray." Nay, much less, because, while we are in a church, we may turn our thoughts to other subjects, and contrive to forget that God is looking on us; but that will not be possible in heaven.

What is amusing about this parrying of the man of the world's objection to "rigid" holiness is its appeal to common sense, a common sense which most men of the world naturally claim to respect. Yet Newman drives home the practical nature of his argument even more insistently:

> We see, then, that holiness, or inward separation from the world, is necessary to our admission into heaven, because heaven is *not* heaven, is not a place of happiness *except* to the holy ... Nay, I will venture to say more than this;—it is fearful, but it is right to say it;—that if we wished to imagine a punishment for an unholy, reprobate soul, we perhaps could not fancy a greater than to *summon it to heaven*. Heaven would be hell to an irreligious man.[41]

Too little is made of Newman's wonderful sense of humor. Here it might be deployed for a very serious purpose, but it is still amusing. He says, addressing an English audience fabled for its insularity,

> We know how unhappy we are apt to feel at present, when alone in the midst of strangers, or of men of different tastes and habits from ourselves. How miserable, for example, would it be

---

[40] Gilbert Keith Chesterton, *Heretics* (1905), in *Collected Works of Gilbert Keith Chesterton, Volume I: Orthodoxy, Heretics and Blatchford Controversies*, ed. David Dooley (San Francisco: Ignatius Press, 1986), 127.
[41] *PPS*, I, sermon 1, 7.

> to have to live in a foreign land, among a people whose faces we never saw before, and whose language we could not learn. And this is but a faint illustration of the loneliness of a man of earthly dispositions and tastes, thrust into the society of saints and angels. How forlorn would he wander through the courts of heaven! He would find no one like himself; he would see in every direction the marks of God's holiness, and these would make him shudder.[42]

This may be funny, but it is also terrifying. Certainly, it is difficult to read without asking ourselves whether we too will turn out like Newman's self-satisfied Mr. Podsnap, finding heaven full of insufferable foreigners. Writing as he does *cor ad cor*, Newman always makes a personal appeal to his readers, and here is no exception.[43] Newman's sermons urge us to recognize the transformative force of quotidian holiness, to make consistency in holiness the pattern of our lives. After all, this is what he did himself. We could be here for days citing passages that bear this out, for Newman's work is a treasure trove of saintly witness, saintly guidance, saintly discipline. Indeed, his very conversion was the result of saintly personal influence. What is that passage from his letters where he speaks of Blessed Dominic Barberi?

> Certainly, Fr Dominic of the Mother of God was a most striking missioner and preacher and he had a great part in my own conversion and in that of others. His very look had a holy aspect which … most singularly affected me, and his remarkable *bonhomie* in the midst of his sanctity was in itself a real and holy preaching. No wonder, then, I became his convert and penitent.[44]

---

[42] Ibid., 7–8.
[43] Newman took his motto, *Cor ad cor loquitur* ("Heart speaks to heart") from St. Francis de Sales (1567–1622), whose understanding of sanctity was rooted, like Newman's, in the affections. "Often make acts of love of Our Lady, the saints, and the holy angels," he once enjoined a correspondent. "Make friends with them. Talk with them frequently, using words of praise and tenderness. When you have gained familiar access to the citizens of the heavenly Jerusalem above, you will grieve far less at bidding farewell to those of the mean city here below." Francis de Sales "To a Lady Who Feared Death" (April 7, 1617), from *A Selection from the Spiritual Letters of St. Francis de Sales* (London: Rivingtons, 1871), 171. For an excellent essay on Newman's motto, see Huw Twiston Davies, "*Cor ad cor loquitur*: What does the Papal Visit Motto Really Mean?" *Catholic Herald* (August 13, 2010).
[44] John Henry Newman to Cardinal Parocchi (October 2, 1889), in *LD*, XXXI, 277.

Barberi personifies the influence Newman extolls in his Oxford University sermon "Personal Influence, the Means of Propagating the Truth" (1832), when he speaks of "the natural beauty and majesty of virtue, which is more or less felt by all but the most abandoned." And here he was careful to stress that he was referring to the living, breathing article, not "virtue in a book." Why?

> Men persuade themselves, with little difficulty, to scoff at principles, to ridicule books, to make sport of the names of good men; but they cannot bear their presence: it is holiness embodied in personal form, which they cannot steadily confront and bear down: so that the silent conduct of a conscientious man secures for him from beholders a feeling different in kind from any which is created by the mere versatile and garrulous Reason.[45]

We have another example still of Newman's appreciation of the force of holiness from a sermon entitled "Christ Hidden from the World" (1837) which, again, nicely contrasts those who choose to reject God's commandments with those who make up their minds and their hearts to obey them. "There are a number of persons who are in no sense irreligious, or open to serious blame, who are very much like each other at first sight, yet in God's eyes are very different," Newman says,

> I mean the great mass of what are called respectable men, who vary very much: some are merely decent and outwardly correct persons, and have no great sense of religion, do not deny themselves, have no ardent love of God, but love the world; and, whereas their interest lies in being regular and orderly, or they have no strong passions, or have early got into the way of being regular, and their habits are formed accordingly, they are what they are, decent and correct, but very little more.[46]

In *The Idea of a University* (1873), Newman would say the same of the English gentleman: he is a fine and respectable figure, but "the creation, not of Christianity, but civilization."[47] Saints, on the other hand, may "look just the same to the world," but "in their hearts" they "are very different," though this difference is often inconspicuous.

---

[45] *Fifteen Sermons Preached in the University of Oxford*, 72–3.
[46] *PPS*, IV, sermon 16, 243.
[47] John Henry Newman, *The Idea of a University*, ed. I. T. Ker (Oxford: Oxford University Press, 1976), 174.

> They make no great show, they go on in the same quiet ordinary way as the others, but really they are training to be saints in Heaven. They do all they can to change themselves ...[48] to obey God, to discipline themselves, to renounce the world; but they do it in secret, both because God tells them so to do, and because they do not like it to be known.[49]

Here is the quintessential Newman. All his life, he was training to be a saint in heaven. And if we want to follow his example, we could do worse than read his edifying sermons.

---

[48] Here, Newman's insistence that we must change if we are to become saints is clear enough. Yet, his understanding of the nature and the advisability of change when it comes to Church doctrine is often misrepresented, especially by Modernists for whom the principle of *semper eadem* is naturally obnoxious. When it comes to change and the development of doctrine, it is always salutary to quote Newman fully, not out of context. Here is the full quotation from *An Essay on the Development of Doctrine* (1845), from which an ill-fated sentence is often misleadingly plucked:

> whatever be the risk of corruption from intercourse with the world around, such a risk must be encountered if a great idea is duly to be understood, and much more if it is to be fully exhibited. It is elicited and expanded by trial, and battles into perfection and supremacy. Nor does it escape the collision of opinion even in its earlier years, nor does it remain truer to itself, and with a better claim to be considered one and the same, though externally protected from vicissitude and change. It is indeed sometimes said that the stream is clearest near the spring. Whatever use may fairly be made of this image, it does not apply to the history of a philosophy or belief, which on the contrary is more equable, and purer, and stronger, when its bed has become deep, and broad, and full. It necessarily rises out of an existing state of things, and for a time savours of the soil. Its vital element needs disengaging from what is foreign and temporary, and is employed in efforts after freedom which become more vigorous and hopeful as its years increase. Its beginnings are no measure of its capabilities, nor of its scope. At first no one knows what it is, or what it is worth. It remains perhaps for a time quiescent; it tries, as it were, its limbs, and proves the ground under it, and feels its way. From time to time it makes essays which fail, and are in consequence abandoned. It seems in suspense which way to go; it wavers, and at length strikes out in one definite direction. In time it enters upon strange territory; points of controversy alter their bearing; parties rise and around it; dangers and hopes appear in new relations; and old principles reappear under new forms. It changes with them in order to remain the same. In a higher world it is otherwise, but here below to live is to change, and to be perfect is to have changed often.

John Henry Newman, *An Essay on the Development of Christian Doctrine* (Notre Dame, IN: University of Notre Dame Press, 1989), 39–40.

[49] *PPS*, IV, sermon 16, 243.

"Heart Speaks to Heart"

One concluding point. Gathered together this evening at this at once joyous and dismaying time, many of us are necessarily concerned about the Church, our beloved Church, which continues to suffer appalling betrayal, turmoil and disgrace. That a kind and solicitous Providence has given us St. John Henry Cardinal Newman as an antidote to these melancholy developments we can have no doubt. Still, it is interesting to see him prefiguring what is now his own saintly charge in one of his most moving sermons "Mysteries in Religion" (1834), in which he writes,

> Christ went to intercede with the Father: we do not know, we may not boldly speculate,—yet, it may be, that Saints departed intercede, unknown to us, for the victory of the Truth upon earth; and their prayers above may be as really indispensable conditions of that victory, as the labours of those who remain among us. They are taken away for some purpose surely: their gifts are not lost to us; their soaring minds, the fire of their contemplations, the sanctity of their desires, the vigour of their faith ... were not given without an object.[50]

In the sermon on saintliness from which I have already quoted, Newman expands on this charge of the saints, which can only strengthen us in our present discontents:

> Very various are the Saints, their very variety is a token of God's workmanship; but however various, and whatever was their special line of duty, they have been heroes in it; they have attained such noble self-command, they have so crucified the flesh, they have so renounced the world; they are so meek, so gentle, so tender-hearted, so merciful, so sweet, so cheerful, so full of prayer, so diligent, so forgetful of injuries; they have sustained such great and continued pains, they have persevered in such vast labours, they have made such valiant confessions, they have wrought such abundant miracles, they have been blessed with such strange successes, that they have been the means of setting up a standard before us of truth, of magnanimity, of holiness, of love. They are not always our examples, we are not always bound to follow them; not more than we are bound to obey literally some of our Lord's precepts, such as turning the cheek or giving away the coat ... but, though not always our examples, they are always our standard of right and good; they are raised up to be monuments and lessons, they remind

---

[50] *PPS*, II, sermon 18, 214.

Newman and the Standard of Saintliness

> us of God, they introduce us into the unseen world, they teach us what Christ loves, they track out for us the way which leads heavenward.[51]

Here is a nice distillation of Newman's standard of saintliness, and it is one under which we can all continue to fight the good fight. The saint in Newman, ever mindful of practicalities, ever distrustful of unreality, does not simply share this standard with us: he teaches us how we can make it our own, and I am sure all of you this evening recall those sterling words from one of his greatest sermons, "Unreal Words" (1839), with which I shall conclude:

> What I have been saying comes to this:—be in earnest, and you will speak of religion where, and when, and how you should; aim at things, and your words will be right without aiming. There are ten thousand ways of looking at this world, but only one right way. The man of pleasure has his way, the man of gain his, and the man of intellect his. Poor men and rich men, governors and governed, prosperous and discontented, learned and unlearned, each has his own way of looking at the things which come before him, and each has a wrong way. There is but one right way; it is the way in which God looks at the world. Aim at looking at it in God's way. Aim at seeing things as God sees them. Aim at forming judgments about persons, events, ranks, fortunes, changes, objects, such as God forms. Aim at looking at this life as God looks at it. Aim at looking at the life to come, and the world unseen, as God does. Aim at "seeing the King in his beauty." All things that we see are but shadows to us and delusions, unless we enter into what they really mean.
>
> It is not an easy thing to learn that new language which Christ has brought us. He has interpreted all things for us in a new way; He has brought us a religion which sheds a new light on all that happens. Try to learn this language. Do not get it by rote, or speak it as a thing of course. Try to understand what you say. Time is short, eternity is long; God is great, man is weak; he stands between heaven and hell; Christ is his Saviour; Christ has suffered for him. The Holy Ghost sanctifies him; repentance purifies him, faith justifies, works save. These are solemn truths, which need not be actually spoken, except in the way of creed or of teaching; but which must be laid up in the heart. That a thing is true, is no reason that it should be said, but that it should be done; that it should be acted upon; that it

---

[51] *Discourses Addressed to Mixed Congregations*, 101–2.

should be made our own inwardly. ... Let us receive the truth in reverence, and pray God to give us a good will, and divine light, and spiritual strength, that it may bear fruit within us.[52]

---

[52] *PPS*, V, sermon 3, 45.

4

Newman and the Italians

How Italy and her People Brought Newman to a New Holiness

Jo Anne Cammarata Sylva

JOHN HENRY NEWMAN always knew how important holiness was for a person to see the Lord. As he said in volume one of the *Parochial and Plain Sermons*,

> One principal test of our being true servants of God is our wishing to serve Him better; and be quite sure that a man who is contented with his own proficiency in Christian holiness, is at best in a dark state, or rather in great peril ... Many men, it is true, are contented with partial and indistinct views of religion, and mixed motives. Be you content with nothing short of perfection; exert yourselves day by day to grow in knowledge and grace; that, if so be, you may at length attain to the presence of Almighty God.[1]

Therefore, for Newman to attain true holiness, he would have to exert himself constantly to grow in knowledge and grace. Yet, as Ian Ker has said, "The story of John Henry Newman's conversion to Catholicism is not quite the same as the story of his discovery of Catholicism ... Now while Newman knew a very great deal about the early Church, he knew extraordinarily little about contemporary Catholicism, apart from its formal doctrines and teaching."[2]

---

[1] John Henry Newman, "Holiness Necessary for Future Blessedness," in *Parochial and Plain Sermons* (London: Longmans & Green, 1907), I, sermon 1, 1.
[2] Ian Ker, *The Catholic Revival in English Literature, 1845–1961* (Notre Dame, IN: Notre Dame University Press, 2003), 13.

Therefore, I will assert that Newman learned many aspects of Catholic tradition and spirituality from his Italian friends—such knowledge which would allow him to grow in holiness so that he could sincerely embrace the fullness of the Catholic faith. These people, two Italian saints and four contemporary Italians, provided him with an understanding of Catholicism that he could not seem to obtain from his own people and his own country.

Growing up, John Henry Newman knew nothing about Catholic culture, and that was the norm. Even in much of twentieth-century English literature, Catholicism was a mystery. Born in 1919 of Welsh descent, Meriol Trevor described her early spiritual life as having been conducted against an intellectual, humanistic background. After the war, she volunteered for relief work and was sent to the Abruzzo and, through this remote area of Italy, she came into contact with a deeply rooted Catholic culture. In her words, "Out of it I have come to Christ." She was especially drawn by the "entirely natural way of praying."[3] As late as the 1970s, Barbara Pym has her characters speak in hushed tones about the scary possibility that one of their acquaintances might have "gone over to Rome." Thus, for many generations, most British people knew nothing about Catholic tradition, the Catholic priesthood, and exactly what Catholic worship was all about. Remember, when he was young, Newman was convinced that the pope was the "Antichrist predicted by Daniel, St. Paul, and St. John."[4] But, if possible, less was known about the character of the Italian people. Too often, they were stereotyped as outrageous thieves who happened to live in a pleasant climate and, somehow, had produced good artwork and music.

Therefore, Newman was fourteen when he first made mention in writing of an Italian personage in a letter to his sister Harriet. "Hang that old monk Alfieri. A great fool writes tragedies and is therefore jealous at anything sublime for fear it should eclipse his own. A great fool of a monk dares to slander the high, lofty magnificent fame of the high lofty magnificent Virgil."[5] Ker's notes to New-

---

[3] Meriol Trevor, *Shadows and Images* (San Francisco: Ignatius Press, 2012), vii–viii.

[4] See www.newmanreader.org > works > arguments > antichrist > lecture 3.

[5] John Henry Newman to Harriet Newman (December 12, 1815) in Charles Steven Dessain *et al.*, eds., *The Letters and Diaries of John Henry Newman*, vols. I–XXXII (Oxford and London: Thomas Nelson, 1961–2007), I, 18 (hereafter *LD*).

man's *Letters and Diaries* add: "Count Vittorio Alfieri (1749–1803), Italian tragic dramatist. He was not a monk."[6] Remember also, Newman's early antipathy to Catholics was so clearly expressed in the *Apologia*:

> There was a Catholic family in the village, old maiden ladies we used to think; but we knew nothing about them. I have of late years heard that there were one or two Catholic boys in the school; but we were carefully kept from knowing this, or the knowledge of it made simply no impression on our minds. My brother will best witness how free the school was from Catholic ideas.[7]

Thus, on his first trip to Italy in 1832, Newman carried with him a prejudice against both Italians and Catholics. And yet, despite his determination to avoid Italians at all costs, he seemed to have been drawn to them and their holiness. By the time he left Italy, Newman had made the discovery of a highly practical and useful kind of religion. Instead of something supernatural, far removed from the ordinary mundane world, Italian Catholicism was a much more spiritual religion than that of the Church of England, which seemed, paradoxically, a far more matter-of-fact kind of "business."[8]

This holy, spiritual, and all-encompassing religion was what Newman craved and, from that point on, the Catholicism of John Henry Newman and the Catholicism of St. Alfonso Liguori, Bl. Dominic Barberi, Alessandro Manzoni, Bl. Antonio Rosmini, Fr. Giovanni Perrone, and St. Philip Neri would be forever intertwined. An Italian, Cardinal Capecelatro, best explained this unique relationship when he gave a commemoration speech shortly after Newman's death in these words:

> In sum, Newman has been at the same time English and Italian; an excellent Englishman, observing the character and rare qualities of his race, he has spread among his people a new light of truth and love; an excellent Italian because from the Vicar of Christ, who is in the midst of our Italy, he has drawn firmness of belief and likewise, with a loving intellect and with a life of holiness, has defended and reinvigorated among us as well that faith which conquers every error, that faith which is sublime

---

[6] *Ibid.*, note by editor, 18.
[7] John Henry Newman, *Apologia pro Vita Sua*, ed. Ian Ker (London: Penguin Books, 1994), 24.
[8] Ker, *The Catholic Revival*, 20.

to us. Furthermore, the learned and saintly English Oratorian has been Italian and one of us ... because he had a particular love of Italy ... Therefore, my dearest children, let us consider Cardinal Newman to be one of us.[9]

How did Newman become "one of us" as the Italians continue to believe him to be? As Newman said, he needed to exert himself to grow day by day to attain holiness, and, while years would pass before he could accept the Church of Rome as his own, his early experiences in Italy gave him an opportunity to witness personally the kindliness and holiness of individual Italians.

During his first visit to Rome, he was certainly carrying with him the idea that Italian Catholics had destroyed the pureness of the Church of Christ; but, at the same time, he was certainly impressed with the beauty of the individual churches. As Newman described this ambivalence to John Frederic Christie,

> Well then, again after this, you have to view Rome as a place of religion—and here what mingled feelings come upon one. You are in the place of martyrdom and burial of Apostles and saints—you have about you the buildings they saw—and you are in the city to which England owes the blessing of the gospel—But then on the other hand the superstitions; or rather, what is far worse, the solemn reception of them as an essential part of Christianity.[10]

But then Newman went off to Sicily where the savage and untamed beauty of the land made a deep impression upon him. In fact, at Taormina, he said that the view from the ancient theatre was "a nearer approach to seeing Eden" than anything he had conceived possible. "I felt for the first time in my life with my eyes open that I must be better and more religious, if I lived there."[11] However, once again, he was greatly disturbed by the people themselves, finding them lacking in both cleanliness and sincere holiness. Then, gradually, the people of Italy began to find a place in his heart. In fact, during that first trip, there were individual acts of holiness that would long remain in his memory.

---

[9] Cardinale Alfonso Capecelatro, "Commemorazione del Cardinale Enrico Newman," speech given to the Confratelli dell'Oratorio di Napoli, November 6, 1890 (Napoli: Tipografia dell'Accademia Reale delle Scienze, 1890), 4–5.

[10] John Henry Newman to John Frederic Christie (March 7, 1833), in *LD*, III, 240–1.

[11] John Henry Newman to Harriett Newman (April 25, 1833), in *LD*, III, 303.

He would never forget his loyal travel companion, Gennaro, upon whom he was totally dependent during his illness. This Italian man would remain etched in his mind and heart as no other: "I left Gennaro at Palermo; he was to go back to Naples to his wife and family ... He was humanly speaking the preserver of my life, I think. What I should have done without him, I cannot think. He nursed me as a child. An English servant never could do what he did."[12]

This important acknowledgement by Newman that an Italian could be more caring and receptive to helping others than even one from his own country was further enforced by other people whom he had met. Throughout the journey, the Italians were polite and helpful despite their poverty, and Newman appreciated what he saw of them: "Dirt, but simplicity and contentment." Douglas Sladen, who met Newman in his later years, said, "Newman liked the Sicilians very much," but he further explained that Newman felt that the dirt was not for want of washing their clothes but, on the contrary, was from the hardscrabble lives that they were forced to live.[13] And there were others. Newman had only good things to say about the owner of the inn where he stayed in Castro Giovanni. His host, Luigi Vestivo, tried to do everything possible on behalf of the stranger from England. On his return home, Newman sent Vestivo, in response to his request, a Bible, presumably in the Authorized Version, accompanied by a letter. "What impressed Newman deeply, apart from their kindness, was the absolute honesty of his host and of all who looked after him."[14]

Even the Italian doctor who attended him during his illness was to make a lifelong impression upon the Englishman. Newman had only picked up a smattering of the Italian language during his travels, and the doctor spoke no English. So together they utilized both Latin and Italian, writing down the exchange. "The paper on which they jotted down their questions and answers, Newman brought back with him to England, and preserved to the end of his life."[15] Newman would remain fascinated with the Italian language,

---

[12] John Henry Newman, *Autobiographical Writings*, ed. Henry Tristram (New York: Sheed & Ward, 1957), 138.
[13] Douglas B. W. Sladen, *In Sicily, 1896–1898–1900* (New York: E. P. Dutton, 1901), 357.
[14] Newman, *Autobiographical Writings*, 113–14.
[15] Ibid., 114.

and he made many attempts to become fluent. Years later, he and St. John would tease each other about their ability to communicate: As he wrote to Dalgairns, "By the bye, you may like to know how St J gets on with Italian." He went on to say that St J had told an Italian that he would meet him in *inferno* (hell) instead of *inverno* (winter) pronouncing f for v.[16] Dante would probably have enjoyed this unexpected visitor to his domain!

At last, having been saved from death and enlightened by God's will, John Henry Newman left Italy on June 13, 1833. Because of his experiences in that beautiful land, his life would never be the same. He had begun to know the Italian people and had gained an understanding of their willingness to put aside their own self-interests to grow in holiness as they followed God's commandments. He even remarked that a new and large sphere of action had opened for him from the very moment of his return. At the same period of time, Newman was having his on-going correspondence with Father Charles Russell who would contribute greatly to Newman's eventual conversion to the Catholic Faith. As Newman said in the *Apologia*,

> He sent me at different times several letters; he was always gentle, mild, unobtrusive, uncontroversial. He let me alone ... He also gave me one or two books ... a volume of St. Alfonso Liguori's Sermons was another ... Now it must be observed that the writings of St. Alfonso, as I knew them by the extracts commonly made from them, prejudiced me as much against the Roman Church as anything else, on account of what was called their "Mariolatry," but there was nothing of the kind in this book. I wrote to ask Dr. Russell whether anything had been left out in the translation; he answered that there certainly were omissions in one Sermon about the Blessed Virgin.[17]

Russell further explained that certain devotions were appropriate in Italy which would not be acceptable to other parts of the world. But, even that Newman began to understand better when he later added, "It is unfair then to take one Roman idea, that of the Blessed Virgin, out of what may be called its context."[18]

For the first time in his life, Newman was reading a more complete version of the works of Liguori, whose life spanned virtually

---

[16] John Henry Newman to J. D. Dalgairns (October 18, 1846), in *LD*, XI, 262.
[17] John Henry Newman, *Apologia*, 179.
[18] Ibid., 180–1.

the whole of the eighteenth century, from his birth in 1696 to his death at the age of ninety-one in 1787, just fourteen years before Newman's birth. The historical records at Naples, where he lived and worked for the greater part of his life, are extensive. In fact, the houses in which he lived, the cathedrals and rural churches where he preached as both priest and bishop, are to a large extent still in existence. He wrote extensively, and a considerable portion of his works is still extant in manuscript form with Alfonso's corrections.[19] From what he now read, Newman was especially taken with the realization that Liguori was a master of anecdotal information which he used to increase the piety of the Italian people. He included commonplace stories to emphasize the powers of Mary.[20]

A Liguori scholar, Reverend Giovanni Velocci, C.SS.R. (Redemptorist), explained the significance of St. Alfonso Liguori in the development of Newman's thoughts:

> Newman knew that this saint was held by Anglicans to be the greatest representative of devotional Catholicism, of Mariolatry, and that Saint Alphonsus had fed his prejudices against Catholicism. But this book was a surprise and a revelation: Newman did not find in it the exaggerated devotions that he feared, but on the contrary a serious and concrete doctrine, even if presented with the mentality and warmth of an Italian ... Newman, his whole life long, maintained a certain debt of gratitude to Saint Alphonsus, because he had received from him a decisive impetus to detach himself from Anglicanism and to orient himself toward the Catholic Church in order to enter into the fullness of light and truth.[21]

Even though by the early 1840s, Newman was on his "death bed" regarding his belonging to the Anglican Church; in true Newman fashion, he also expressed hope in the future with the acknowledgement that Fr. Russell had introduced him to Liguori. Coincidentally, at that same time, there was in England an Italian Passionist priest, Father Dominic Barberi, and, from the first, Newman was inspired by Barberi's holiness. He commented about Barberi's missionaries who were coming to his own country: "If they want to

---

[19] Frederick M. Jones, ed., *Alphonsus de Liguori: Selected Writings* (New York: Paulist Press, 1999), 9.
[20] *Ibid.*, 259.
[21] Giovanni Velocci, *Newman: Il coraggio della verità* (Vatican City: Libreria Editrice Vaticana, 2000), 199–214.

convert England, let them go preach to the people like St. Francis Xavier—let them be pelted and trampled on, and I will own that they can do what we cannot. I confess they are our betters, by far."[22]

And they were indeed "pelted and trampled on" when Fr. Dominic Barberi appeared on the scene in November of 1840. Born in a small Italian village in 1792, he was already forty-eight when he undertook such an arduous assignment. He and his few missionaries were among the first in England since the Reformation to wear religious habits, and they were constantly reminded that their actions inflamed hostility towards them. During Holy Week one year, Barberi preached "exactly as in Italy," which included wearing a habit with the crucifix on the breast. "Timid Catholics used to implore him to avoid such provocation, but he preferred to listen to those who told him that 'the wearing of the sandals seemed to give great edification,' and advised him 'to wear both habit and sandals on all future occasions of the kind.'"[23]

In midsummer of 1844, Barberi gave a mission in a hayloft in a location not far from Littlemore, and this proximity was the opportunity that the Italian had been waiting for to pay a visit to Newman and his community. Newman wrote long after: "His very look had about it something holy. When his form came in sight, I was moved to the depths of my being in the strangest way."[24] Fr. Barberi was so different from the Anglican priests that he was being recognized as a threat to the Protestants. In his words, "They preach in their churches at the same hour as I do, to keep people from hearing me. They have started house to house visiting, with the sole object of exhorting people not to come to me. I hear that they are afraid and have some idea that I am a very learned person."[25]

Of course, although he was simple and unaffected, Dominic was not shy, and he took this first meeting as an opportunity to further his relationship with the residents of Littlemore. Because of both his holiness and tenacity, Fr. Dominic Barberi was the one who, on the evening of October 9, 1845, received John Henry Newman into the "one Church and the one Communion of Saints." The Italian

---

[22] Barberi, quoted in Denis Gywnn, *Father Dominic Barberi* (Buffalo: Desmond, 1948), iii.

[23] *Ibid.*, xiv.

[24] John Henry Newman, quoted in Meriol Trevor, *Newman: The Pillar of the Cloud* (New York: Doubleday, 1962), 324.

[25] Barberi, quoted in Gwynn, *Father Dominic Barberi*, xv–xvi.

was overjoyed and humbled that he should have been the personage to convert Newman, but he was also taken with the genuine character of the man.[26] And, likewise, Newman would write long afterwards about Barberi: "His very look had about it something holy. When his form came in sight I was moved to the depths of my being in the strangest way."[27]

However, the strain of so many trials, sufferings, and endeavors in a foreign country wore out the strength of Father Dominic Barberi. In one of his last letters before his death, he wrote that there were already three Passionist houses in England. He had in residence twenty-eight religious, of whom eleven were already priests. They had by that time given two-hundred and fifty missions, a hundred of which Father Dominic had written and delivered himself. They had converted numerous Protestants to Catholicism and brought thousands of lapsed Catholics back to the Faith. Personally, Father Dominic had received John Henry Newman into the Church of Rome. But, by summer of 1849, he realized that he "had finished his course." Within less than a month, Father Dominic Barberi collapsed on a train on his way back to his new foundation in London, and he died within a few hours on August 27, 1849.[28]

Newman was deeply saddened by the passing of Barberi and would praise "the little Italian" for the rest of his life. But he was now faced with the prospect of becoming a Catholic priest, and he had certainly not known many of them. But, ironically, he would be most inspired not by an actual priest but a fictional character created by Alessandro Manzoni, the man who wrote *I promessi sposi*, which I like to refer to as the *Moby Dick* of Italy.

Catholic priesthood had come for Newman on May 30, 1847 and, when he wrote to Pope Pius IX just three weeks after his ordination, he proudly called himself in Italian, "il sacerdote Giovanni Maria Newman."[29] But he needed to find a model for the kind of priest that he wanted to be and the form of ministry in which he and his fellow converts would engage. In 1837, he wrote to his sister Jemima that he had just read a book that she had mentioned and that he was captivated by its spirituality: "I have lately been reading a

---

[26] Barberi, quoted in Gwynn, *Father Dominic Barberi*, 140.
[27] John Henry Newman, quoted in *Newman: The Pillar of the Cloud*, 324.
[28] Gwynn, *Father Dominic Barberi*, xix.
[29] John Henry Newman to Pope Pius IX (June 20, 1847), in *LD*, XII, 87.

novel you spoke of, *I Promessi Sposi*, and am quite delighted with it ... It is most inspiring—it quite transported me in parts."[30]

Newman did not lose interest in Manzoni and *I promessi sposi*, and he would mention them time and again. In late 1839, when he was in despair over the perplexing situation for priests in England, he expressed his confusion to Frederic Rogers: "Can the R.C.s have any tender feeling towards Anglicanism? Who among us ever showed them any kindness? What are the R.C.s to admire in us? our married Bishops or our Dissenting brethren? I cannot deny that my heart is with neither of these." In such difficult times, Newman found solace and hope by thinking of Rome and, most specifically, of bringing to mind Manzoni's Italian monk, Fra Cristoforo, a true example of how a priest of God should live a holy life. In the same letter, he added, "The Capuchin in *Promessi Sposi* has struck in my heart like a dart. I have never got over him. Only I think it would be, in sober seriousness, far too great an honour for such as me to have such a post, being little worthy or fit for it."[31]

There were several aspects of Fra Cristoforo which immediately appealed to Newman. Cristoforo was a Capuchin who had resurrected himself from an earlier dissipated existence to live a life of total devotion to God and His people. Newman definitely found himself attracted to the monk's holy life. "The Capuchins owned nothing, wore a dress more strikingly different from other men than the other orders, made a more open profession of humility and in all these ways exposed themselves more openly to both the veneration and the vilification which such things attract from men of various dispositions and various opinions."[32] In addition, there was something so personally compelling about the manner in which Manzoni described the transformation of a "cocky young aristocrat named Lodovico who killed a man in a duel to settle the vain question of a right-of-way by a stone wall into the very complex and saintly Fra Cristoforo, a man whose duties were those of preaching and of the tending of the dying, which he carried out willingly and conscientiously."[33]

---

[30] John Henry Newman to Mrs. John Mozley (October 6, 1837), in *LD*, VI, 150.
[31] John Henry Newman to Frederic Rogers (September 15, 1839), in *LD*, VII, 151.
[32] Alessandro Manzoni, *The Betrothed* [*I promessi sposi*], ed. & trans. Bruce Penman (London: Penguin, 1972), 73.
[33] *Ibid.*, 90–1.

Newman was to indicate often that this manner in which Cristoforo spent out his life was the ideal for a Catholic priesthood which should directly serve the people of God, even though he felt himself little worthy or fit for it. And because Newman had this connection with the fictional priesthood of Cristoforo, he was most anxious to meet Alessandro Manzoni, his Italian creator. In fact, when he was planning for his trip to Italy in 1846, he mentioned in a letter to Edward Badeley, "I propose to go to Manzoni." [34] But, much to Newman's regret, the meeting never took place and, in an October letter to Dalgairns from Milan, he said, "We have missed Manzoni—but been lionized almost daily by his chaplain, Ghianda, whom we like very much." [35]

Newman missed Manzoni, but he would always remember Milan as a most wonderful place. In his words, "Here were St. Ambrose, St. Augustine, St. Monica, St. Athanasius." Further, he found what he felt was a real Catholic religion practiced in a real Catholic country by real Catholic people. He had a sincere feeling that this holiness permeated every aspect of Italian life: "It is really wonderful to see this Divine Presence looking out almost into the open streets from the various churches, so that at St. Laurence's we saw the people take off their hats from the other side of the street as they passed along; no one to guard it, but perhaps an old woman who sits at work before the church door, or has some wares to sell." [36]

During the same trip to Milan in 1846 when he missed meeting Manzoni, Newman was also trying to come into contact with another luminary, Antonio Rosmini-Serbati. Born in Northern Italy in 1797, Rosmini was a philosopher, patriot, and promoter of the Catholic revival in Italy, and he founded the Institute of Charity, or Rosminians, in 1828. The field of work during his lifetime lay almost exclusively in Italy and England, and he and his followers established Ratcliffe College near Loughborough, England. In Rome, today, there is a Collegio Rosmini, and there are Rosmini houses around the world. These institutes are constantly promoting the Cause for the Beatification of Rosmini:

---

[34] John Henry Newman to Edward Badeley (August 8, 1846), in *LD*, XI, 219.
[35] John Henry Newman to J. D. Dalgairns (October 18, 1846), in *LD*, XI, 262.
[36] John Henry Newman to Henry Wilberforce (September 24, 1846), in *LD*, XI, 252.

> He heard God's call at a young age and became a priest in 1821. He devoted his considerable academic gifts to the service of God and the Church. Pope Pius VIII told him in 1829 that God was calling him to write books ... Rosmini remained faithful to this particular vocation despite difficulties and misunderstandings his works sometimes provoked ... With his wide-ranging intellect, Rosmini tackled the leading questions in theology and philosophy of his day. Alessandro Manzoni, the most famous Italian writer of the time and Rosmini's close friend, said of him: "He is one of the six or seven brightest minds that honour humanity."[37]

Newman's letters indicate that, quite early in the 1840s, he was aware of Antonio Rosmini and his priests. He was to visit Ratcliffe College quite often, and in January of 1846, he and St. John spent the Feast of the Epiphany with the Rosminians. When Newman was explaining options that he was considering for the future, he discussed the success of the Rosminians whom he felt were spreading their holiness throughout England by means of education and practice.

In 1846 letters to both Church and Dalgairns, he praised this unique work of the Rosminians (to which he could personally relate) by saying that he saw "nothing except that the notion of a theological school is a great idea—and natural, not only from our hitherto line of reading, but because the Rosminis ... are fast spreading themselves, as givers of retreats and missions, all over England."[38]

One can understand why Newman felt a connection with Antonio Rosmini, as he also was a philosopher, a writer, and a priest. Also, like Newman, Rosmini had had an education which included a study of both the Church Fathers and the luminaries of the Enlightenment. A twentieth-century leader of the Rosminians, Father General Giuseppe Bozzetti, has characterized Rosmini as an Italian intellectual who respected and understood the foremost philosophical minds of his era, and yet his modern outlook never diminished the true holiness that comes from one's following the Catholic Faith. "Like Newman, he was a man for whom all that was thought or felt could not be seen or understood except in the light and love of the Christ-God. One of the greatest Christians of his time, what was peculiarly his was a capacity for including

---

[37] Father James Flynn, *Antonio Rosmini: Man of God* (Rome: Collegio Rosmini, n.d.), 4.
[38] John Henry Newman to J. D. Dalgairns (July 6, 1846), in *LD*, XI, 196.

everything in his religious vision without in any way changing a single essential characteristic of what he saw."[39]

Although Newman and Rosmini never met in person, they would forever be linked together for several obvious reasons. They were both embodiments of Newman's *Meditation on God's Providence*: "He may take away my friends, He may throw me among strangers, He may make me feel desolate, make my spirits sink, hide the future from me—still He knows what He is about."[40] Newman found an example of a man who underwent great trials and even condemnation because of what some considered his "modern" tendency to address reason and religion. As Newman explained to Dalgairns in 1846, "We heard in Milan that Rosmini's one *idea* was to make a positive substantive philosophy instead of answering objections in a petty way, and being no more than negative. He seemed to think the age required a philosophy, for at the present there was none. Several things of the same kind, that he said, struck me as good."[41]

As they both had been scrutinized and criticized in life, so would they both be lauded many years after. In Pope John Paul II's encyclical letter *Fides et Ratio*, the Holy Father stated:

> We see the fruitful relationship between philosophy and the Word of God in the courageous research pursued by more recent thinkers, among whom I gladly mention, in a Western context, such as John Henry Newman and Antonio Rosmini … One thing is certain: attention to the spiritual journey of these masters can only give greater momentum to both the search for truth and the effort to apply the results of that search to the service of humanity."[42]

Alessandro Manzoni and Antonio Rosmini were definitely positive influences upon Newman; but, unfortunately, he never got to meet them during his first trip to Italy as a Catholic. However, there were two other Italians whom he did encounter (one personally and one through his followers) during those same years, and they would be forever praised by him for their holiness. The first was Giovanni

---

[39] Giuseppe Bozzetti, quoted in Claude Leetham, *Rosmini: Priest, Philosopher and Patriot* (London: Longmans, Green: 1957), xvii.
[40] John Henry Newman, *Meditations and Devotions* (London: Longmans, Green: 1916), 420.
[41] John Henry Newman to J. D. Dalgairns (In fest. S. Caecil, 1846), in *LD*, XI, 279.
[42] Pope John Paul II, *Fides et Ratio*, no. 74, September 15, 1998.

"Heart Speaks to Heart"

Perrone, a contemporary theologian who became his friend and advisor, and the other was St. Philip Neri, the sixteenth-century Christian humanist who would be his inspiration for becoming an Oratorian. While St. Philip was the ideal, Perrone was the real-life figure to whom Newman would turn when he arrived in Rome. This man, who would first offer help during those early days in Italy and for the remainder of their lives, was one of the most famous theologians of that era. Father Giovanni Perrone was a Jesuit whose longevity (1794–1876) almost mirrored that of Newman.

Newman was to learn about Perrone even before he went to Italy. As he was preparing to be a student at the College of Propaganda, he wrote in a letter to St. John that there was much practical and educational advice that they should follow:

> You may not have *clothes* of your own—the Rector takes away coat, trousers, shirts, stockings, etc. etc. and gives you some of the Propaganda's ... They give you two cassocks, an *old* one and a new one ... Yes, they are there from all nations—except English. Dr. F. said there was not a single Englishman all the time he was there. To complete it, he said that I shall be kept there three years, and that I should have to read Perrone.[43]

From those first days at Propaganda, Newman needed knowledge in several areas of his Catholic learning, including the development of doctrine and the importance of reason in connection with a true faith, and he understood that he could not get such knowledge in England:

> The Jesuit Perrone ... would have furnished the only, or almost only, example of a Catholic thinker who was not a mere amateur ... How was Tradition to be preserved in a world where all the schools that had ensured its continuity, at all events since the Middle Ages, had been expelled or abolished? Within this general framework, the position of the Catholic Church in England was peculiar. There it had suffered more grievously in the past than in any other land ... Debarred from the universities, unable to give their priests a worthy cultural education, they lived as it were on the fringe of the world, clinging like wild creatures to the protection of a sort of ghetto, which, even when the chance was given them, they showed no disposition to quit.[44]

---

[43] John Henry Newman to Ambrose St. John (July 8, 1846), in *LD*, XI, 200–1.
[44] Louis Bouyer, *Newman: His Life and Spirituality* (New York: P. J. Kennedy, 1958), 347–8.

Therefore, with priesthood looming before him and with his lack of exposure to Catholic theologians in England, Newman desired a connection with Perrone. Most especially, Newman was having controversy about the publication of his *Essay on the Development of Doctrine*. As he explained, "I am so timid about my *Essay* that I have not the heart to hasten its publication until I have a little more encouragement that I am not ... in material heresy."[45] In the Spring of 1847, a troubled Newman sent Perrone a list of formal propositions summarizing his views on faith and reason and, most especially, a paper on his theory of development. As he explained, "I am sending you herewith those things that you have asked from me ... If by little notes in the margins ... you would add your judgments to my labors, it would be a gain to me ... This only will I profess, I am able to err, but I do not wish to be a heretic."[46]

Newman made a summary in Latin of his views on the development of doctrine, and then Father Perrone added his own comments. From a thorough analysis of the "Paper on Development," one can see Perrone's objective:

> There is a well-known fact that Newman did not as a rule propound his theology in technical terms. At the beginning of the theological studies which he undertook in Rome, he took great pains to master scholastic terminology, and Perrone tried to bring Newman's very personal way of expressing himself into line with the language of the schools.[47]

In later years, the Newman-Perrone friendship did not diminish and, in 1867, they exchanged further correspondence. The letter from Perrone was written in Italian and expressed his continued support for his English friend: "I suppose that Your Reverence has not forgotten our lovely Italian language so I am writing you a few lines in this tongue. And first, I thank you for the happy memory that you have continued to keep of me. You cannot believe how much I have always loved and esteemed your Reverence." And Newman responded in Latin because he did not feel competent enough in Italian:

---

[45] John Henry Newman to J. D. Dalgairns (February 14, 1847), in *LD*, XII, 3.
[46] John Henry Newman to Father Perrone, S.J. (Spring, 1847), in *LD*, XII, 40.
[47] Gunter Biemer, *Newman on Tradition* (New York: Herder, 1967), 169.

> For who am I, that after so many years I am still in your memory
> and heart ... While I am always aware that I am not a theologian,
> I certainly try to the best of my ability to treat the theological
> matters in my books in a zealous, accurate and cautious way.
> I rejoice greatly now to be thought of as having written on
> those matters so as to seem to have pleased, not myself alone,
> but also you.[48]

The second voyage to Italy in 1846 was very fortuitous, for not only did Newman become a lifelong friend to Perrone, he also became much more familiar with St. Philip Neri and the Oratory that he had instituted. Newman's discovery of Neri would create a unique combination—a nineteenth-century Englishman and a sixteenth-century Italian. Together, they made each other known and respected throughout the world. By the time Newman came on the scene, Neri was already widely revered in Italy. Born in Florence in 1515, Neri had had both scholastic and pastoral successes before the Feast of Pentecost in 1544, when he received the miraculous gift of the Holy Ghost and the palpitation of his heart.[49] There is evidence that Newman was aware of Neri and his work even before he came to Rome for that visit. In a letter to Faber, he said, "I have long felt special reverence and admiration for the character of St. Philip Neri, as far as I knew it, and was struck by your saying that his church at Rome was at Vallicella—I wish we could all become good Oratorians but that, I suppose is impossible."[50]

But such a goal was possible and, by the end of 1846 and after numerous visits to the Chiesa Nuova, Newman had made up his mind. He formally asked the Pope for permission to erect an Oratory in Birmingham, England, as well as in other cities. According to Father Dessain, Newman found in the Italian saint

> a holiness adapted to the modern age, our age, something that
> could be really and genuinely put into practice, not an artificial
> imitation of the piety of past ages—and yet it must be the holiness
> of the New Testament, something all-absorbing and leading on
> through detachment to complete surrender to God. Newman
> thought he found all this in Saint Philip.[51]

---

[48] Giovanni Perrone/John Henry Newman, "The Newman–Perrone Paper on Development," ed. T. Lynch, *Gregorianum* 16 (1935), 445–6.
[49] V. J. Matthews, *St. Philip Neri* (London: Burns & Oates, 1934), 12.
[50] John Henry Newman to F. W. Faber (February 1, 1846), in *LD*, XI, 105.
[51] C. S. Dessain, "Cardinal Newman's Attraction to St. Philip," *Oratorium* (1970),

And the way of St. Philip would constantly lead Newman onward. Later in life, even when his youthful enthusiasm had greatly diminished, he would write poems about the importance of the Italian saint in his life:

> *So now, with his help, no cross will I fear,*
> *But will linger resign'd through my pilgrimage here,*
> *A child of St. Philip, my master and guide,*
> *I will live as he lived, and will die as he died.*[52]

I have spoken at length about how the Italians made Newman more holy by explicating Catholic tradition, but they themselves greatly respected this British cardinal. His Italian friends treasured him always and were proud of his many achievements. He was delighted when the Romans showed their love for him by enthusiastically welcoming him to their city in May of 1879. His *Biglietto* speech was a great success, and the Italians responded with great aplomb to both Newman's ideas and his persona. Father Thomas Pope recounted their reaction to the new English cardinal: "All has passed off beautifully—an immense crowd—the Father made a very fine speech … which is very heartily enjoyed here … The Italian ladies behind me were unanimous that he was: '*che bel vecchio! Che figura!*' etc., etc. '*Pallido si, ma bellissimo!*'"[53]

With the love and support of his Italian friends—most especially, St. Alfonso Liguori, Bl. Dominic Barberi, Alessandro Manzoni, Bl. Antonio Rosmini, Fr. Giovanni Perrone, and St. Philip Neri—Newman was able to grow in holiness and to say his motto in relatively good Italian—IL CUORE PARLA AL CUORE!

POSTSCRIPT

I feel that I was fated to write about Newman and Italy. My father was born and grew up in Sicily, a few kilometers away from Castro Giovanni in the foothills of Mount Etna. My doctorate from an American university was modeled after the Doctor of Letters

---

71.
[52] John Henry Newman, *Verses on Various Occasions* (London: Burns & Oates, 1883), 310.
[53] Father Thomas Pope quoted in Wilfred Ward, *Life of Newman* (London: Longmans, Green, 1912), II, 463.

"Heart Speaks to Heart"

degree established by the University of Oxford in 1900. During my studies, I took a course in Newman and became fascinated with how well he could connect with people—whether it be by means of sermons, personal correspondence, or even poems and novels. I can read and write Italian and have translated the Italian writings into English. In fact, I spent time at the Vatican library working through the old Italian texts. In pursuit of Newman, I have traveled to Rome, Sicily, Casa Manzoni in Milan, Villa Manzoni in Lecco, Littlemore, and Oxford. And, lastly, my son is a priest who studied at Louvain and lived for nine years in Rome.

5

"The Value of One Single Soul"

Newman on the Gravity of Sin
and the Quality of Mercy

Ryan Marr

WHEN DISCUSSING THE TOPIC OF CONSCIENCE, John Henry Newman warned of a counterfeit understanding of it, which he described as the right of self-will. Today, we hear much talk of mercy. Yet, in this area as well, there is the risk of adopting a false understanding of mercy—one divorced from a realistic perception of sin and blind to the urgency of sanctification. Although Newman did not explicitly address the notion of "counterfeit mercy," he did provide sufficient warnings against just such an outlook at various places in his writings.[1] Thus, Newman's works continue to serve as an important resource for keeping in view a proper sense of the seriousness of sin as an offense against God's justice, as well as the transformative power of divine mercy. In a multitude of ways, Newman demonstrates how God's mercy does not merely declare us innocent but sets us free so that our lives take on the shape and character of Christ's own. My chapter will offer a preliminary sketch of Newman's insights on these matters, concluding with an application of his ideas to contemporary debates around the reception of Holy Communion.

---

[1] See, for example, his sermon on "The Religion of the Day" in *Parochial and Plain Sermons* (1869; reprint New York: Longmans, Green & Co. 1907), I, sermon 24, 309 ff. (hereafter *PPS*).

"Heart Speaks to Heart"

NEWMAN ON THE GRAVITY OF SIN

More so than many theologians of our day, Newman possessed a strong sense of the gravity of human sin in the light of God's absolute holiness. One of Newman's more striking comments on this topic can be found in Lecture Eight of his *Lectures on Certain Difficulties Felt by Anglicans in Submitting to the Catholic Church*, where he contrasts the vocation of Christ's Church with the normal concerns of "men of the world." Newman remarks,

> The Church aims, not at making a show, but at doing a work. She regards this world, and all that is in it, as a mere shade, as dust and ashes, compared with the value of one single soul. She holds that, unless she can, in her own way, do good to souls, it is no use her doing any thing; she holds that it were better for sun and moon to drop from heaven, for the earth to fail, and for all the many millions who are upon it to die of starvation in extremest agony, so far as temporal affliction goes, than that one soul, I will not say, should be lost, but should commit one single venial sin … She considers the action of this world and the action of the soul simply incommensurate, viewed in their respective spheres.[2]

This excerpt expresses just how seriously Newman viewed sin as an offense against God's just ordering of the world. The mission of the Church, he asserts, can only properly be understood in light of the wound that sin has afflicted. As the Body of Christ in the world, the Church's mission is fundamentally oriented to the salvation of sinners and thus incommensurate with projects of mere societal progress. In the quote above, Newman frames the matter starkly. The Bride of Christ would rather humanity suffer the most extreme agony than that one person commit even a single venial sin.

The popular religion of the day—what Newman deemed the "religion of civilization"—simply could not comprehend this way of approaching world affairs. In the eighth discourse of his *The Idea of a University*, Newman forcefully drove this point home by contrasting the core teachings of the Catholic faith with the values of the popular religion of the day. As a "system of pastoral instruction and moral duty," Catholicism teaches, among other points,

---

[2] John Henry Newman, *Lectures on Certain Difficulties Felt by Anglicans in Submitting to the Catholic Church* (1850; reprint New York: Longmans, Green & Co., 1901), 239–40.

the ruined state of humanity, our utter inability to gain heaven by our own powers, the moral certainty of losing one's soul apart from divine assistance, the simple absence of all rights and claims on the part of the creature in the presence of the Creator, and the imperative and obligatory force of the voice of conscience.[3] These were not central concerns of the liberal or latitudinarian outlook that had taken root in the Church of England—an outlook which had no real place in its theology for penance or corresponding notions regarding the spiritual benefits of self-mortification.[4] One could see this dynamic, Newman argued, at work in the British educational system, which was concerned not with producing saints, but gentlemen—productive members of polite society who respect piety and devotion, who perhaps even support religious institutions, but who did not take too seriously the more radical teachings of Christ. In contrast to latitudinarian interpretations of the Christian life, Newman consistently kept the Gospel demand of perfection at the fore of his theology.

Thus, even though Newman's vision of holiness took on nuanced shades at different points in his life—as John Connolly has convincingly demonstrated[5]—there was an underlying continuity in his writings on this topic: namely, the urgency attendant upon all Christians to seek total sanctification whatever the costs. The centrality of this theme to his theological outlook can be seen in his very earliest works: for example, in the initial selection of his *Parochial and Plain Sermons*—"Holiness Necessary for Future Blessedness"—wherein Newman notes that, "The whole history of redemption, the covenant of mercy in all its parts and provisions, attests the necessity of holiness in order to be saved; as indeed even our natural conscience bears witness also."[6] In this sermon,

---

[3] John Henry Newman, *The Idea of a University Defined and Illustrated*, ed. Martin Svaglic (1858; repr. Notre Dame, IN: Univ. of Notre Dame Press, 1982), 139.

[4] For background to the latitudinarian outlook, as manifested in the thought of Renn Dickson Hampden, see Robert Pattison, *The Great Dissent: John Henry Newman and the Liberal Heresy* (Oxford: Oxford University Press, 1991), 80–5. Cf. E. McDermott, "Latitudinarianism," in *New Catholic Encyclopedia* (New York: McGraw-Hill, 1967), VIII, 522.

[5] John R. Connolly, "Newman's Vision of Holiness in the World," in *Newman and Life in the Spirit: Theological Reflections on Spirituality for Today*, ed. John Connolly and Brian Hughes (Minneapolis, MN: Fortress Press, 2014), 145–65.

[6] John Henry Newman, "Holiness Necessary for Future Blessedness," in *PPS*, I, sermon 1, 1.

it is clear that, for Newman, holiness is no mere pious sentiment. Rather, true holiness entails circumcision of heart, total separation from sin, a love of God's commandments, and hatred of the works of the world, the flesh, and the devil—in short, to live one's life with eternity in view, detached from the normal concerns of human society, as if one were already dead.[7]

In pointing all of this out, Newman recognizes that some of his readers will be skeptical of the idea that the Christian life demands such severity. But, such skepticism, Newman notes, misunderstands the nature of our reconciliation with God, which is not something imposed upon us from the outside, but an authentic transformation of our very being, so that in body, mind, and spirit we are prepared to experience eternal blessedness in union with the Thrice-Holy God. In other words, in order to experience the Beatific Vision, we must first be made entirely holy. This movement—from a state of perdition to being filled with the Holy Spirit and drawn up into the divine life—is not something voluntaristically carried out against our will; rather, it involves the free response of human beings to the gift of prevenient grace which, of course, precedes but does not coerce the act of faith. In this light, even if a person who is still attached to sin could hypothetically enter heaven, he would be utterly miserable there. Thus, as Newman sums up the matter, "it would be no mercy to permit him to enter."[8] Severity in religious practice is not a hindrance to happiness; rather, it is the very means by which we are purged of our attachment to sin and thereby prepared for a life of unending beatitude in heaven.

THE GOSPEL OF GRACE, WHERE MERCY AND JUSTICE MEET

Newman's vision of what holiness entails is conceptually rooted in his understanding of divine justice. Regarding this latter topic, one of the central texts is the sixth of his *Oxford University Sermons*, entitled "On Justice, as a Principle of Divine Governance." Here, Newman contrasts the Christian position with the outlook of those "who take a favourable view of human nature, as it actually is

---

[7] See *ibid.*, 2–3.
[8] *Ibid.*, 3

found in the world, and of the spiritual condition and the prospects of mankind."[9] At a surface level, these persons have a great deal of evidence in support of their perspective, for "certainly the face of things is so fair, and contains so much that is interesting and lofty," that those in the world "may be pardoned" for believing them "to be as cheerful and as happy as they appear."[10] The primary difficulty with this conclusion, however, is that the revealed Word of God attests otherwise. Or, as Newman puts it, "it *would* be commendable, did not Scripture acquaint us from the very first (by way of warning, previous to our actual experience) with the deceitfulness of the world's promises and teaching."[11]

"But is not the Gospel a message of glad tidings, a proclamation of peace, and source of joy?" the astute reader might ask. Yes, Newman rejoins, but these truths "must never be separated from the bad tidings of our fallen nature."[12] The fundamental error of false prophets is to proclaim "peace, peace" when there is no peace. In this instance, Newman aims his sights on the false prophets of Socinianism. According to Newman's diagnosis, the "essential dogmas" of this heresy are as follows:

> that the rule of Divine government is one of benevolence, and nothing but benevolence; that evil is but remedial and temporary; that sin is of a venial nature; that repentance is a sufficient atonement for it; that the moral sense is substantially but an instinct of benevolence; and that doctrinal opinions do not influence our character or prospects, nor deserve our serious attention.[13]

In short, Socinian theology emphasizes God's loving kindness to such an extent that it obscures God's justice, ultimately advancing what amounts to a formally Pelagian soteriology.

But, as Newman goes on to show, both natural reason and Sacred Scripture testify against this viewpoint. On the level of human reason, the instinct for justice is as natural to us as the conviction that there is an underlying benevolence driving the course of history.

---

[9] John Henry Newman, "On Justice, as a Principle of Divine Governance," in *Fifteen Sermons Preached before the University of Oxford between A.D. 1826 and 1843* (1871; reprint London: Rivingtons, 1890), 99.
[10] Ibid.
[11] Ibid.
[12] Ibid., 101.
[13] Ibid., 104.

Thus, while we may naturally wish others well, we also naturally "feel indignation when vice triumphs" and are unsettled until injustices are rectified. In the spiritual life, "as we grow in habits of obedience," our sense of the eternal justice of God—rather than diminishing—becomes even more real and immediate to us. In fact, far from being a source of unremitted fear, the rule of justice represents a kind of anchor to the person of faith: "taking us even as we are," Newman writes, "much as each of us has to be forgiven, yet a religious man would hardly wish the rule of justice obliterated. It is a something which he can depend on and recur to; it gives a character and a certainty to the course of Divine Governance."[14] In sum, the error of Socinianism is what Newman calls a "theory of God's *unmixed benevolence*."[15] In contrast, the orthodox position understands the "rule of mercy" as "the supplement, not the substitute of the fundamental law of justice and holiness."[16] And when the reality of divine mercy is kept in view, the rule of justice does not influence us to despair, but, instead, produces thoughts of consolation and hope—as the lives of the saints attest.[17]

In Newman's vast body of writings, perhaps no other piece more memorably expresses his thoughts on these topics than the second sermon in his *Discourses Addressed to Mixed Congregations*. The language of mercy pervades this sermon. We see here, though, that mercy does not mean God overlooks our sins, but that He patiently waits for us to turn from them and gives us the power to do so if we will avail ourselves of His grace. Newman points to different biblical examples to press this point. In the age of Abraham, for example, the people who inhabited the promised land were already involved in heinous sins, yet God did not expel

---

[14] *Ibid.*, 114.
[15] *Ibid.* (emphasis added).
[16] *Ibid.*
[17] Newman comments: "In proportion as we grow in habits of obedience, far from our vision of the eternal justice of God vanishing from our minds, and being disowned by our feelings, as if it were but the useful misconception of a less advanced virtue, doubtless it increases, as fear is cast out. The saints in heaven ascribe glory to God, 'for true and righteous are His judgments.' 'Great and marvelous are Thy works, Lord God Almighty; just and true are Thy ways, Thou King of saints.' If, then, the infinite benevolence of God wins our love, certainly His justice commands it; and were we able, as the Saints made perfect are able, to combine the notion of both in their separate perfections, as displayed in the same acts, doubtless our awe and admiration of the glorious vision would be immeasurably increased." *Ibid.*, 107-8.

them from the land immediately. "Why?" Newman asks. "Because God's mercies were not yet exhausted."[18] Similarly, in the case of the impious Prince Belshazzar, the Scripture records a long track record of grievous faults: drunkenness, adulteries, concubinage, pride, cruelty, excessive taxation, and much else. This went on for many years, "till at length he exhausted the Divine Mercy, and filled up the chalice of wrath."[19]

Catholics who excuse their sins, by passing them off as minor or by assuming that some later day will be provided for repentance, toy with the same trap that ultimately snared the Canaanites and Belshazzar. The sin of presumption ignores the fact that we do not control the future and have no way of knowing when we will be called before the judgment seat of Christ. Newman warns his listeners: "No; you cannot decide, my brethren, whether you are outrunning God's mercy, merely because the sin you now commit seems to be a small one; it is not always the greatest sin that is the last."[20] Furthermore, the Creator allots different lengths of life to each person; no one can ultimately determine when or how she will die. Thus, "no one can promise himself that he shall have time for repentance" in the future.[21] As Sacred Scripture reminds us, "Behold, now is the acceptable time; today is the day of salvation" (1 Cor 6:2). Putting off repentance, then, involves a counterfeit understanding of divine mercy. We are criminals, Newman writes, and are not fit to adjudicate our own case. But so many of us fail to admit this: we are prideful and reticent to entertain the idea of judgment for ourselves. Newman concludes: "For all these reasons, we have no real idea what sin is, what punishment is, and what grace is. We do not know what sin is, because we do not know what God is; we have no standard with which to compare [sin], till we know what God is"—both in His mercy and in His justice.[22]

It would be misleading, however, to end this section on what might be perceived as a threatening note. The sin of despair presents

---

[18] John Henry Newman, *Discourses Addressed to Mixed Congregations* (1849; reprint Notre Dame, IN: University of Notre Dame Press, 2002), 28.
[19] "His hour came: one more sin he [committed], and the cup overflowed; vengeance overtook him on the instant, and he was cut off from the earth." Ibid., 29.
[20] Ibid., 30.
[21] Ibid., 32.
[22] Ibid., 33.

a danger equal to that of presumption. The key, ultimately, is that God does not stand against us, but is for us. To paraphrase St. Paul, the Gospel brought by Jesus Christ is "not 'Yes' and 'No'; but in him it is always 'Yes.' For all the promises of God find their 'Yes' in him" (2 Cor 1:19–20a). For Newman, this truth is rooted in the reality that God does not simply declare us innocent in a juridical sense, but truly makes us righteous, renewing our entire selves through the indwelling of the Holy Spirit. God's mercy means that no human word can condemn us: "Let he who is without sin cast the first stone" (Jn 8:7). God's grace means that the Spirit empowers us to turn from sin: "Go and sin no more" (Jn 8:11). And, a sound comprehension of Scripture helps us to recognize that this is a journey, beginning with our regeneration through baptism and continuing until we reach total conformity to Christ and are united with God in the beatific vision.

IMPLICATIONS FOR TABLE DISCIPLINE AND EUCHARISTIC FELLOWSHIP

Newman's insights on these matters, I would contend, are instructive for thinking through recent theological discussions regarding Eucharistic fellowship. In the last few years, Pope Francis' ministry has sparked a reassessment of certain disciplines related to the reception of Holy Communion. While much of the debate has focused on the Apostolic Exhortation *Amoris Laetitia*, the Holy Father had given indications prior to the release of this document that he was considering an alteration to the Church's discipline. The heart of Pope Francis' vision is expressed in his oft-repeated remark that the Eucharist "is not a prize for the perfect but a powerful medicine and nourishment for the weak."[23] The implications of this assertion became the source of serious debate during the Extraordinary Synod on the Family in 2014. While the Synod Fathers addressed a number of topics, media attention concentrated in large part on whether the Holy Father and other

---

[23] See, e.g., Pope Francis, *Evangelii Gaudium*, no. 47; http://w2.vatican.va/content/francesco/en/apost_exhortations/documents/papa-francesco_esortazioneap_20131124_evangelii-gaudium.html.

bishops were pressing for a liberalization of the traditional teaching that remarried Catholics were to be barred from Communion.

The final outcome of these debates did not usher in clearly defined juridical norms. Rather, Pope Francis merely signaled a change in pastoral practice, without spelling out concrete directives of how this change should be implemented. In paragraph 305 of his Post-Synodal Exhortation, Francis wrote that, "Because of forms of conditioning and mitigating factors, it is possible that in an objective situation of sin—which may not be subjectively culpable, or fully such—a person can be living in God's grace, can love and can also grow in the life of grace and charity, while receiving the Church's help to this end."[24] The footnote to this remark clarified that the Church's pastoral accompaniment in such cases can, sometimes, include the help of the sacraments, and here Francis reiterated that the Eucharist is medicine for the weak, not a prize for the perfect.[25] Discernment around this matter, Pope Francis counseled, need not take place in semi-public contexts such as ecclesiastical tribunals, but could be navigated in the internal forum: that is, in confidential conversations between laypersons and their priest.[26]

Numerous commentators praised Pope Francis' boldness on these matters, seeing in these sections of *Amoris Laetitia* a concrete instantiation of the Gospel of mercy, which has been a central theme

---

[24] *Amoris Laetitia*, no. 305, http://w2.vatican.va/content/dam/francesco/pdf/apost_exhortations/documents/papa-francesco_esortazione-ap_20160319_amoris-laetitia_en.pdf.

[25] Cf. Thomas D. Williams in Crux (Oct. 22, 2015): "This beautiful expression is both a rebuke to the proud and an encouragement for those who acknowledge their unworthiness to receive Holy Communion, which Catholics believe to be the real body and blood of Jesus Christ. Who, after all, on careful self-examination, finds himself to be truly 'worthy' to receive the Lord in Holy Communion? The Eucharist is no gold star on the forehead of 'good' Christians, but an undeserved gift to strengthen pilgrims who stumble along through life with their gaze fixed on heaven. As the great doctor of the Church St. Ambrose wrote: 'If, whenever Christ's blood is shed, it is shed for the forgiveness of sins, I who sin often, should receive it often: I need a frequent remedy." Thomas D. Williams, "The Eucharist: A Prize for the Just or Medicine for Sinners?" https://cruxnow.com/church/2015/10/22/the-eucharist-a-prize-for-the-just-or-medicine-for-sinners/.

[26] See *Amoris Laetitia*, no. 300: "Conversation with the priest, in the internal forum, contributes to the formation of a correct judgment on what hinders the possibility of a fuller participation in the life of the Church and on what steps can foster it and make it grow."

of Francis' pontificate.[27] There is a tension here, however, in that the Catholic tradition has consistently held that communicants must be in a state of grace before receiving Holy Communion. This discipline was grounded in the Pauline warning against partaking of the Body and Blood of the Lord unworthily. As a safeguard against profaning the Body and Blood of Christ, St. Paul teaches that anyone who approaches the table should examine himself or herself first, for to commune in an unworthy manner entails eating and drinking judgment upon oneself (see 1 Cor 11:27–9). Pope Francis, of course, recognizes this facet of the Catholic tradition, as is clear from paragraph 47 of his encyclical *Evangelii Gaudium* in which he comments that, "Everyone can share in some way in the life of the Church … nor should the doors of the sacraments be closed for simply any reason."[28] By adding the phrase "for simply any reason," Francis points to the reality that there can be reasons for counseling someone to abstain from Holy Communion, but that perhaps these reasons have been applied too rigorously.

The conversation today remains open-ended. In fact, individual dioceses and bishops' conferences in different parts of the world have implemented divergent pastoral guidelines in response to Pope Francis' exhortation.[29] I am under no illusions that my brief presentation could resolve the complex debates surrounding *Amoris Laetitia*, but I do contend that Newman's theology, treated above, has an important contribution to make to these conversa-

---

[27] Pope Francis has lauded the work of Cardinal Walter Kasper as inspiration for the pastoral orientation of his pontificate. See Walter Kasper, *Mercy: The Essence of the Gospel and the Key to Christian Life*, trans. William Madges (Mahwah, NJ: Paulist Press, 2014). Cardinal Kasper directly addresses the question of mercy in relation to marital difficulties in *The Gospel of the Family*, trans. William Madges (Mahwah, NJ: Paulist Press, 2014). For a critique of Kasper's theology of mercy, see Daniel P. Moloney, "What Mercy Is," *First Things* 251 (March 2015), 60–2.

[28] *Evangelii Gaudium*, no. 47.

[29] Contrast, for example, Archbishop Charles Chaput's directives with the practices pursued by the Argentine and Maltese bishops. See E. Christian Brugger, "The Catholic Conscience, the Argentine Bishops, and *Amoris Laetitia*," *Catholic World Report* (Sept. 20, 2016), http://www.catholicworldreport.com/2016/09/20/the-catholic-conscience-the-argentine-bishops-and-amoris-laetitia/. For an incisive analysis of *Amoris* in light of previously articulated teaching regarding the sacrament of matrimony, see Matthew Levering, *The Indissolubility of Marriage: Amoris Laetitia in Context* (San Francisco, CA: Ignatius Press, 2019).

tions. Amidst the debates around specific pastoral practices, we cannot lose sight of the fact that the free gift of God's mercy fundamentally involves a call to repentance. There are ways, as Pope Francis has warned us, that Christian communities can attempt to limit the extension of divine mercy by unjustly excluding certain persons or groups from fellowship. That being said, the opposite danger exists whereby mercy could be understood as excusing sin, rather than as the invitation to amend one's life.

It is unfortunate that this conversation has fixated on a few very specific moral cases (e.g., cohabitation, remarriage, and, to a lesser extent, same-sex sexual relationships), when the call to turn away from sin in preparation for Holy Communion is a demand placed upon all of us. By focusing on the issue of Communion for remarried Catholics, we perhaps run the risk of failing to pay adequate attention to other serious sins — say, defrauding workers of their wages — that are not frequently dealt with in homilies or spiritual direction. Whatever the case under consideration happens to be, however, we must never lose sight of the fact that objective and unconfessed sins of a serious nature constitute a barrier to receiving the Eucharist. The Church's longstanding discipline with respect to this question is a testament to the Catholic understanding of the Eucharist as a foretaste of heaven. If a person has committed a serious sin, but not yet confessed it, calling them to repentance *is* to be concerned with their ultimate joy. To quote Newman again, "even supposing a man of unholy life were suffered to enter heaven, he would not be happy there; so that it would be no mercy to permit him to enter."[30] To reiterate, since the reception of the Eucharist is a sacramental participation in the future glories of the beatific vision, receiving the Body and Blood of Christ unworthily would not lead to true happiness, but only to further distress. For those who have been civilly remarried after divorce, therefore, the path to receiving Holy Communion necessitates repentance for the remarriage and a commitment by the partners "to live as brother and sister" if the sacramental marriage cannot be repaired.[31] The

---

[30] *PPS*, I, sermon 1, 6.

[31] Cf. Pope John Paul II, *Familiaris Consortio*, no. 84, http://www.vatican.va/content/john-paul-ii/en/apost_exhortations/documents/hf_jp-ii_exh_19811122_familiaris-consortio.html: "Together with the Synod, I earnestly call upon pastors and the whole community of the faithful to help the divorced, and with solicitous care to make sure that they do not consider

same call to repentance confronts all of us who have committed a grave sin of whatever kind and have not confessed it yet.

Admittedly, these are complex matters, and marriages on the ground are not easily or neatly categorized. For instance, there may be a member of the faithful who many years ago remarried with only a vague sense of Catholic sacramental theology and who now desires to conform to the totality of what the Church teaches regarding marriage. One could also point to situations in which one of the spouses in a civil marriage expresses a desire for amendment of life, but the other spouse possesses no such desire. Pope Francis has rightfully challenged priests to accompany such persons on the journey of faith and to do so with their vision constantly directed towards God's merciful love. Nevertheless, this accompaniment must receive its orientation from the Church's teaching that a valid marriage is indissoluble, and therefore that remarriage is contrary to God's design for human relations.[32] In our present historical context, Newman's writings serve as a helpful guide for re-receiving this truth, in that he sets before us a stark depiction of the gravity of human sin and never allows this concept to be obscured by a sentimentalized understanding of mercy. As St. James attests, "Mercy triumphs over judgment" (James 2:13). We mistake that mercy for a counterfeit idea if we fail to see that God extends it to us precisely in order that we might fulfill the entirety of the Law of Christ out of love for our merciful Savior (cf. 1 Cor 9:21 and John 14:21).

---

themselves as separated from the Church, for as baptized persons they can, and indeed must, share in her life ... However, the Church reaffirms her practice, which is based upon Sacred Scripture, of not admitting to Eucharistic Communion divorced persons who have remarried. They are unable to be admitted thereto from the fact that their state and condition of life objectively contradict that union of love between Christ and the Church which is signified and effected by the Eucharist. Besides this, there is another special pastoral reason: if these people were admitted to the Eucharist, the faithful would be led into error and confusion regarding the Church's teaching about the indissolubility of marriage."

[32] For an overview of the biblical and theological reasons for the traditional discipline, see the essays in Robert Dodaro, ed., *Remaining in the Truth of Christ: Marriage and Communion in the Catholic Church* (San Francisco, CA: Ignatius Press, 2014).

6

To Witness the Unseen

Sanctity in the Thought of John Henry Newman and Wilfrid Ward

Elizabeth A. Huddleston

While we look not at the things which are seen, but at the things which are not seen; for the things which are seen are temporal, but the things which are not seen are eternal.

2 Corinthians 4:18

Now faith is the assurance of things hoped for, the conviction of things not seen. For by it the men of old received divine approval. By faith we understand that the world was created by the word of God, so that what is seen was made out of things which do not appear.

Hebrews 11:1–3

IN HIS 1855 NOVEL *Callista: A Sketch of the Third Century*,[1] John Henry Newman described the main character's first introduction to the Christian Gospel as not just an experience of reading a static text, but as an experience of a living and personal God. As Callista opened and began to read the parchment containing the Holy Gospel that she had been harboring under her girdle, a transformation occurred in her. As she read the "simple" and "elegant" "provincial Greek" addressed to Theophilus,[2] she

---

[1] John Henry Newman, *Callista: A Sketch of the Third Century* (London: Burns & Lambert, 1855). Newman republished it under the same title in 1881, and then the book was later reissued under the more familiar title, *Callista: A Tale of the Third Century* (London: Longmans, Green & Co., 1901). Unless otherwise noted, the original 1855 version of the novel is cited in this article.

[2] In this description, Newman was referencing the Gospel of Luke (and Acts), which is addressed to "Theophilus," which means "Friend of God" (see Lk 1:3, Acts 1:1).

became "absorbed in the volume," and began to realize that what she had been gifted "was simply a gift from the unseen world."[3]

The Gospel, for Callista, "opened a view of a new state and community of beings, which only seemed too beautiful to be possible."[4] This "new state," as Newman described in his novel, was not just a new state "of things," but as a "presence of One who was simply distinct and removed from anything that she [Callista] had, in her most imaginative moments, ever depicted to her mind as ideal perfection."[5] Callista recognized in her conscience that what she experienced in her imagination was a real, or actual, experience of the person of Christ:

Here was that to which her intellect tended [the Gospel], though that intellect could not frame it. It could approve and acknowledge when set before it what it could not originate. Here was He who spoke to her in her conscience; whose Voice she heard, whose Person she was seeking for. Here was He who kindled a warmth on the cheek of both Chione and Agellius. That Image sank deep into; she felt it to be a reality. She said to herself, "This is no poet's dream; it is the delineation of a real individual. There is too much truth, and nature, and life, and exactness about it, to be anything else."[6]

Newman's description of Callista's exposure to the Gospel, which was published ten years after Newman's own conversion to Roman Catholicism, demonstrates his commitment to a notion of sanctity in which a person's perception of the unseen, or invisible, world grows more substantial and clearer as he or she more fully experiences God within the human faculties of imagination and conscience. Newman's description of Callista's conversion to the Gospel also demonstrates Newman's Neo-Platonic understanding of the invisible world as being more "real" than what we experience in our material world, which led Newman to explore how humans are able to experience the divine world, which exists beyond our sensory experience. This exploration resulted in some of Newman's most profound theological ideas of both the Church's reception of divine revelation and the more individual notion of how human persons encounter the divine persons.

---

[3] Newman, *Callista*, 252.
[4] Ibid., 252–3.
[5] Ibid., 253.
[6] Ibid.

While a separation between Newman's ecclesiology and his more personal notion of the human experience of the divine is mentioned here, it should be noted that this separation is somewhat artificial because Newman's ecclesiology and his theology of the human person's experience of the divine are intrinsically linked throughout both Newman's Anglican and Catholic writings.

This article explores the notion of "sanctity" through the lens of Newman's theology of how the human imagination and conscience help the Christian striving for sanctity to realize the presence of the invisible world, even though we cannot intuit this presence by means of our senses. Furthermore, this article also explores how this aspect of Newman's thought was received in the writings of Wilfrid Ward, an influential British theologian during the time of the Roman Catholic Modernist Crisis at the turn of the twentieth century.

A SANCTIFIED VIEW OF REALITY

Demonstrated in Callista's comment that the Gospel "is a delineation of a real individual" is Newman's theology that the invisible world is very much alive. Newman's reflection on the invisible world and its relation to us in the material world spans both his Anglican and Catholic writings, though the theological motif was a particularly important one for him as he preached his sermons as an Anglican minister. The Neo-Platonic idea of an invisible world lying hidden beyond the veil of materiality was an important part of his understanding of how we realize God's divine revelation within the Church, as well as how Christians are able to realize the presence of a personal God within their own life of devotion. In his sermon "The Invisible World," for example, Newman argued for a notion that the invisible world is more real than our material world because it is understood as closer and more attuned to the immaterial Triune God.[7] For Newman, divinity is considered as existing more fully than our fleeting material existence.[8] He, for

---

[7] John Henry Newman, *Parochial and Plain Sermons* (London: Longmans, Green & Co., 1907), IV, sermon 13 (hereafter *PPS*).

[8] Newman emphasized this type of Neo-Platonism in his Anglican sermons (pre-1845), particularly in his *Parochial and Plain Sermons* (published 1834–43), *Fifteen Sermons Preached before the University of Oxford* (1826–43), and his

example, wrote that "Almighty God" "exists more really and absolutely than any of those fellow-men whose existence is conveyed to us through the senses."[9]

This invisible world, however, for Newman was not understood as a far-away place, the presence of which Christians are devoid. Rather, in his Anglican sermons, Newman described our material world as participating in the perfect invisible world and vice versa, as well as our world of materiality as fleeting and secondary to the eternality of the invisible transcendent realm of divinity.[10] Newman explained, however, that even though we are not able to experience God physically,[11] we can be sure of God's presence because, as humans created in *imago Dei* (in the image of God), we are able to perceive God in our conscience, which will be discussed in more detail in the following section.

The invisible world for Newman was understood as present here and now, rather than being distant in both time and space.

Sermons on Subjects of the Day (published 1843). However, Newman edited all of these sermons and republished them as a Roman Catholic, thus baptizing, so-to-speak, the theological motifs found in the sermons, most notably here, the invisible worlds theological motif.

[9] PPS, IV, sermon 13, 202. Continuing, Newman preached, "yet we see Him not, hear Him not, we do not 'feel after Him,' yet without finding Him. It appears, then, that the things which are seen are but a part, and but a secondary part of the beings about us, were it only on this ground, that God Almighty, the Being of beings, is not in their number, but among 'the things which are not seen.'" (202)

[10] For excellent expositions into Newman's theology of the invisible world, see Frédéric Libaud, *Voir l'invisible: le monde surnaturel chez John Henry Newman* (Paris: Saint-Léger Éditions, 2016). See also Louis Bouyer, *L'Église de Dieu* (Paris: Les Éditions du Cerf, 1970) and *Newman's Vision of Faith: A Theology for Times of General Apostasy* (San Francisco: Ignatius Press, 1986); Keith Beaumont, *Dieu intérieur: La théologie spirituelle de John Henry Newman*, Études Newmaniennes (France: Éditions Ad Solem, 2014); Benjamin John King, *Newman and the Alexandrian Fathers: Shaping Doctrine in Nineteenth-Century England* (Oxford: Oxford University Press, 2009); Ian Ker, *Newman on Being a Christian* (Notre Dame, IN: University of Notre Dame Press, 1990); John R. Connolly and Brian W. Hughes, eds., *Newman and Life in the Spirit: Theological Reflections on Spirituality for Today* (Minneapolis: Fortress Press, 2014); C. S. Dessain, *The Spirituality of John Henry Newman* (Minneapolis: Winston Press, 1977); Peter C. Wilcox, *John Henry Newman: Spiritual Director 1845–1890* (Eugene, OR: Pickwick Publications, 2013), 44–63; James Arthur and Guy Nicholls, *John Henry Newman* (London: Bloomsbury, 2007), 92; and Robert A. O'Donnell, "The Two Worlds of John Henry Newman," *New Oxford Review* 78, no. 7 (Sept, 2011), 36–8.

[11] As in physically seeing God with our eyes or touching God with our hands.

Newman, for example, preached that "the world of spirits then, though unseen, is present; present not future, not distant. It is not above the sky, it is not beyond the grave; it is now and here; the kingdom of God is among us."[12] Similarly, Newman described the invisible world as not only a reality for the afterlife but in terms of a relationship in which we participate during our finite lives. Newman explained that the invisible world is active and alive alongside our visible world and is able to reveal itself in our religious practice.

For Newman, it was clear that there is more to reality than our senses can reveal: "a world of Saints and Angels, a glorious world, the palace of God, the mountain of the Lord of Hosts, the heavenly Jerusalem, the throne of God and Christ, all these wonders, everlasting, all-precious, mysterious, and incomprehensible, lie hid in what we see."[13] The question, however, is how exactly humans are able to participate and relate to invisible divine reality? First, according to Newman, we participate by virtue of our creation in the image of God, and then more fully by virtue of Christian baptism. Likewise, Newman argued that we are able to participate in the invisible world because we have been grafted more fully into the invisible society when he preached that "The Divine Baptism, wherewith God visits us, penetrates through our whole soul and body. It leaves no part of us uncleansed, unsanctified. It claims the whole man for God. Any spirit which is content with what is short of this ... is not from God."[14]

Though Newman described the invisible world as present all around us, he often conceived of the invisible world in cosmological terms. Newman, for example, in his *Oxford University Sermon* "On the Development of Doctrine," incorporated a cosmological description of the invisible world to explain how persons in the Church, or even the Church herself, are related to divinity in the depths of our being, even though we are bound, at least for now, by our mortality. This patristic notion of the human person as created for communion with both divine and earthly elements is the basis for his understanding of how humans, both collectively

---

[12] *PPS*, IV, sermon 13, 207.
[13] *Ibid.*, 210.
[14] John Henry Newman, *Sermons Bearing on Subjects of the Day*, "Connection between Personal and Public Improvement" (London: Longmans, Green & Co., 1902), sermon 10, 131.

within the Church and individually within our personal devotion, experience the invisible God.[15] For example, after asking, "What science brings so much out of so little? Out of what poor elements does some great master in it create his new world!",[16] Newman argued that "as there is a divinity in the theology of the Church, which those who feel cannot communicate, so is there also a wonderful creation of sublimity and beauty."[17] Newman then provided a description of our human emotions and yearnings as intrinsically and ontologically connected to invisible reality:

> Can it be that those mysterious stirrings of heart, and keen emotions, and strange yearnings, after we know not what, and awful impressions from we know not whence, should be wrought in us by what is unsubstantial, and comes and goes, and begins and ends in itself? It is not so; it cannot be. No, they have escaped from some higher sphere; they are the outpourings of eternal harmony in the medium of created sound; they are echoes from our Home; they are the voice of Angels, or the Magnificat of Saints, or the living laws of Divine Governance, or the Divine Attributes; something are they besides themselves, which we cannot compass, which we cannot utter.[18]

Similarly, in his Anglican sermons, Newman often related the greater cosmos to the cosmos of the heart as a way to connect the human person with invisible reality. It is in the interior heart, or human conscience, that humans experience divinity most closely, according to Newman's Anglican sermons. It is in Newman's relating this greater cosmos and the cosmos of the heart that he incorporated an emphasis on both the transcendence and immanence of God into this understanding of the invisible world. In this theological structure, God is both present in the transcendent cosmological "higher sphere," as well as immanently present within the personal nature of the human conscience. In his sermon

---

[15] For a brief but in-depth explanation of the patristic anthropological mindset, see Nonna Verna Harrison, *God's Many-Splendored Image: Theological Anthropology for Christian Formation* (Grand Rapids, MI: Baker Academic, 2010).

[16] Newman, *Fifteen Sermons Preached before the University of Oxford*, sermon 15: "The Theory of Developments in Religious Doctrine," sermon 15, 345. Newman preached this sermon at the University of Oxford as he neared his conversion to Catholicism in 1845.

[17] Ibid.

[18] Ibid., 346–7.

"The Indwelling Spirit," for example, Newman argued that the interiority of the human person should strive to match the perfect harmonious nature of the invisible cosmos:

> The condescension of the Blessed Spirit is as incomprehensible as that of the Son. He has ever been the secret Presence of God within the Creation: a source of life amid the chaos, bringing out into form and order what was at first shapeless and void, and the voice of Truth in the hearts of all rational beings, tuning them into the harmony with the intimations of God's Law, which were externally made to them ... Doubt, gloom, impatience have been expelled; joy in the Gospel has taken their place, the hope of heaven and the harmony of a pure heart, the triumph of self-mastery, sober thoughts, and a contented mind.[19]

Newman described the Spirit as working interiorly in the human heart to bring it closer into harmony with God. The emotions (passions) of doubt, gloom, and impatience are replaced by virtuous thoughts that correspond with divinity.

Similarly, Newman argued that the goodness in the world extends from divine goodness. This is expressed beautifully in his sermon on the invisible world:

> Bright as is the sun, and the sky, and the clouds; green as are the leaves and the fields; sweet as is the singing of the birds; we know that they are not all, and we will not take up with a part for the whole. They proceed from a centre of love and goodness, which is God himself; but they are not His fulness; they speak of heaven, but they are not heaven; they are but as stray beams and dim reflections of His Image.[20]

As Mark McIntosh observes, "against a post-Lockean landscape, such language can easily sound merely romantic, an escape from a religious discourse becalmed in a little pool of 'evidences' and arguments over logical warrants."[21] However, what Newman

---

[19] *PPS*, II, sermon 19, 218.
[20] *PPS*, IV, sermon 13, 211.
[21] Mark Allen McIntosh, "Newman and Christian Platonism in Britain," *The Journal of Religion* 91, no. 3 (July 2011), 344. McIntosh "considers the implications of Newman's Christian Platonism for his understanding of the natural world and his corresponding anxieties about reductionist epistemologies." Moreover, he reads "Newman against the backdrop of his predecessor Christian Platonists in Britain," which "allows the integration of theology and spirituality in his writing to become both clearer and more explanatory of other facets of his thought" (344–5).

articulated here is related to his anthropological view of divine revelation, which is rooted in ancient Christian anthropology. Namely, this is the idea that God created the world—particularly humanity—in such a way as both to recognize and participate in the divine image, or divine goodness, through signs and symbols prevalent in our material world, such as bread and wine in the Eucharist. Humans, because we are created *imago Dei*, are able to recognize the signs of God within the material world, even though it is understood that the material world is fleeting.

Regarding the personal character of God, in his Anglican sermons, Newman did not categorize human emotion and longing as insignificant in our experience of the divine.[22] Rather, Newman categorized our longing for something greater than ourselves: namely the divine world, as our human nature intrinsically connected with God's same longing for humanity. In other words, we long for God as God longs for us.

Already hinted at in this section is the importance of the human conscience for Newman's theology of how humans, even in our finite state, are able to perceive the inner-workings of the divine world within us as we grow in holiness throughout our lives. Alongside his description of the significance of the invisible world for our knowledge of the presence of God was Newman's explanation of how the human mind and heart, or imagination and conscience, work together to perceive the reality beyond the veil of our senses. While many of Newman's Anglican sermons were dedicated to explaining the significance of the invisible world, his later works tended to focus more explicitly on explaining how we can be certain of the presence of the invisible world, as well as how we can participate more fully in the divine life.

IMAGINATION AND CONSCIENCE

The conscience, according to Newman, is the human faculty that connects us with God. Therefore, a well-formed conscience, or well-tuned conscience, perceives the presence of God more clearly than a conscience that is more focused on worldly things. While Newman mentions this anthropological idea in his Anglican sermons,

---

[22] "Experience of the divine" is my turn of phrase, rather than Newman's.

it is not until his later works after his conversion to Catholicism that he explains most fully his theology of the human conscience.

For Newman, the conscience and the imagination function together in order to allow the person (and Church) to recognize and assent to invisible divinity. Newman wrote, for example, in his *Letter to the Duke of Norfolk* (1875) that

> conscience is the voice of God … Conscience is not a long-sighted selfishness, nor a desire to be consistent with oneself; but it is a messenger from Him, who, both in nature and in grace, speaks to us behind a veil, and teaches and rules us by His representatives. Conscience is the aboriginal Vicar of Christ.[23]

Conscience for Newman is what provides the imagination with an image of God's revelation.

As Frederick Aquino gracefully states, "An important feature of conscience, for John Henry Newman, is the capacity to sense things divine."[24] Newman's contemplation of the communication between the imagination and conscience, much like his contemplation of the invisible world, spanned both his Anglican and Catholic years. However, Newman's most complete theology of the relationship between imagination and conscience resides in his 1870 work *An Essay in Aid of a Grammar of Assent*.

Newman explained the conscience in terms of an analogy between the perception of the visible world versus our perception of the invisible world. Newman argued that as "we have our initial knowledge of the universe through sense, so do we in our first instance begin to learn about its Lord and God from conscience."[25] Similarly, Newman wrote,

> As from particular acts of that instinct, which makes experiences, mere images (as they ultimately are) upon the retina, the means of our perceiving something real beyond them, we go on to draw the general conclusion that there is a vast external world, so from the recurring instances in which conscience acts, forcing upon us importunately the mandate of a Superior, we have fresh evidence

---

[23] Newman, "Letter to the Duke of Norfolk," in *Certain Difficulties Felt by Anglicans in Catholic Teaching*, II, 249.

[24] Frederick D. Aquino, "An Educated Conscience: Perception and Reason in Newman's Account of Conscience," *Studies in the Literary Imagination* 49, no. 2 (Fall 2016), 63.

[25] Newman, *An Essay in Aid of a Grammar of Assent* (London: Longmans, Green & Co., 1903), 63.

> of a Sovereign Ruler, from whom those particular dictates which we experience proceed; so that ... we may, by means of that induction from particular experiences of conscience, have as good a warrant for concluding the Ubiquitous Presence[26] of One Supreme Master, as we have, from parallel experience of sense, for assenting to the fact of a multiform and vast world, material and mental.[27]

The primary question raised here is how the imagination and conscience aid in moving a person from a notional apprehension to a real assent of what cannot be experienced by the senses.[28] Newman asked, for example, "But the question is whether a real assent to the mystery, as such, is possible?" He argued, first, that "it is not possible, because, while we can image the separate propositions, we cannot image them all together." This is because, as Newman explained,

> The mystery transcends all our experience; we have no experience; we have no experiences in our memory which we can put together, compare, contrast, unite, and thereby transmute into an image of the Ineffable Verity;—certainly; but what *is* presented in some degree a matter of experience, what

---

[26] In his sermons, Newman did speak about the "experience" of God as well as "experience" of religion. However, Newman more often used the idea of "God's presence."

[27] Newman, *Grammar of Assent*, 63.

[28] Newman spoke of both notional and real apprehensions and notional and real assents. Regarding a notional apprehension, Newman wrote, referring to our apprehension of "a billion or trillion," that "we can, indeed, have some notion of it, if we analyze it into its factors, if we compare it with other numbers, or if we illustrate it by analogies or by its implications." However, in the "vast number in itself," "we cannot assent to a proposition of which it is the predicate, but we can assent to the truth of it" (*ibid.*, 45). Real apprehension for Newman "is the stronger ... more vivid and forcible." Real apprehension is the "experience of concrete facts." It is the difference between "theory and practice, reason and sight, philosophy and faith." Newman wrote, "Not that real apprehension, as such, impels to action, any more than notional; but it excites and stimulates the affections and passions by bringing facts home to them as motive causes. Thus it indirectly brings about what the apprehension of large principles, of general laws, or of moral obligations, never could effect" (*ibid.*, 11–12). Newman wrote regarding "notional assents" thus: "The assent which we give to mysteries, as such, is notional assent; for by the supposition, it is assent to propositions which we cannot conceive, whereas if we had had experience of them, we should be able to conceive them, and without experience assent is not real" (*ibid.*, 46). Real assents, for Newman, were associated with "Belief" (*ibid.*, 90).

is presented for the imagination, the affections, the devotion, the spiritual life of the Christian to repose upon with a real assent, what stands for things, not for notions only, is each of those propositions taken one by one, and that, not in the case of intellectual and thoughtful minds only, but of all religious minds whatever, in the case of a child or a peasant, as well as of a philosopher.[29]

Newman, however, associated "real assent" with "belief," which he contrasted with the more notional "inference." For example, Newman wrote "while Assent, or Belief, presupposes some apprehension of the things believed, inference requires no apprehension of the things inferred."[30] In other words the distinction between "inference" and "belief" is that "Inference is necessarily concerned with surfaces and aspects; that it begins in itself, and ends with itself; that it does not reach as far as facts; that it is employed upon formulas."[31] Real objects, such as "motives and actions, character and conduct, art, science, taste, morals, [and] religion" are dealt with "not as they are, but simply in its own line, as materials of argument or inquiry, that they are to it nothing more than major and minor premises and conclusions."[32]

However, for Newman, belief, in contrast to inferences, is "concerned with things concrete, not abstract, which variously excite the mind from their moral and imaginative properties."[33] Belief "has for its object, not only directly what is true, but inclusively what is beautiful, useful, admirable, heroic; objects which kindle devotion, rouse the passions, and attach the affections."[34] And thus, belief "leads the way to actions of every kind, to the establishment of principles, and the formation of character, and is thus again intimately connected with what is individual and personal."[35]

For a real assent to occur, Newman argued that there must be an object to which to assent. For invisible realities, Newman

---

[29] Ibid., 130.
[30] Ibid., 90.
[31] Ibid.
[32] Ibid.
[33] Ibid.
[34] Ibid.
[35] Ibid., 91. Newman here was not arguing for an individualistic understanding of belief. Rather, he was contending that the conscience is not simply interested in propositions as they exist in themselves. It is interested in things that matter to the individual or person.

understood the imagination as presenting before the person the object in which to believe, and it is through religious practice and devotion that the object appears more and more real. Newman argued, for example, that "the purpose, then, of meditation is to realize them [the Gospels]; to make the facts which they relate stand out before our minds as objects, such as may be appropriated by a faith as living as the imagination which apprehends them."[36] The role of the conscience, in this instance, is what allows a person certainty that the image produced by the imagination is of divine origins. The imagination, Newman noted, is able to assent to an image to which "no external reality" exists.[37] This is where the well-formed individual conscience is an extension of the communal conscience. Newman, for example, wrote that "strictly speaking, it is not imagination that causes action; but hope and fear, likes and dislikes, appetite, passion, affection, the stirrings of selfishness and self-love."[38] The imagination finds "a means of stimulating those motive powers" and thus provides "a supply of objects strong enough to simulate them."[39] The imagination, however, while individual on the one hand, is deeply communal in its practical experience.

Newman concluded, regarding real assents, that our communal religious practice of "great sensibility, compunction and horror at sin, frequenting the Mass and other rites of the Church, meditating on the contents of the Gospels, familiarity with hymns and religious poems, dwelling on Evidences, parental example and instruction, religious friends, strange providences, powerful preaching," all inform the imagination as to the divine object of worship. While the experience of these, Newman argued, is deeply personal, the "bond of intercourse between those whose minds had been thus variously wrought into a common assent" is "far stronger than could follow upon any multitude of mere notions which they unanimously held."[40] Newman here, in beautiful Victorian prose, was arguing that the collective imagination and the conscience of the Church steeped in millennia of Christian worship provides the individual with the certainty that the object of their worship

[36] Ibid., 79.
[37] See ibid., 80–1.
[38] Ibid., 82.
[39] Ibid., 82.
[40] Ibid., 87.

is in fact the same object presented in the Gospels and worshiped in the Church's liturgies.

For Newman, the human imagination and conscience together are able both to conceptualize and experience divine invisible reality. Benjamin King notes that the Tractarians, of whom Newman was one of the founders, "spoke of the imagination's grace filled *recognition* of God's work."[41] For Newman, the imagination is a human faculty associated with "the apprehension of the 'concrete.'"[42] Similarly, Newman spoke in the *Grammar of Assent* of the imagination as connected with that which is *personal*, which is contrasted with that which is *common*. Newman likewise associated the imagination with *real assents*, which involve the apprehension of images and which are of a *personal character*.[43] Similar to the

---

[41] King, *Newman and the Alexandrian Fathers*, 7, n12. See also Matthew Muller, "Newman's Poetics and the Inspiration of the Bible in *Arians of the Fourth Century*," *Newman Studies Journal* 14, no. 2 (Fall, 2017), 5–24.

[42] See Bernard Dive, *John Henry Newman and the Imagination* (London: T. & T. Clark, 2018), 15.

[43] Newman wrote that real assents

> are of a personal character, each individual having his own, and being known by them. It is otherwise with notions; notional apprehension is in itself an ordinary act of our common nature. All of us have the power of abstraction, and can be taught either to make or to enter into the same abstractions; and thus to co-operate in the establishment of a common measure between mind and mind. And, though for one and all of us to assent to the notions which we thus apprehend in common, is a further step, as requiring the adoption of a common stand-point of principle and judgment, yet this too depends in good measure on certain logical processes of thought, with which we are all familiar, and on facts which we all take for granted. But we cannot make sure, for ourselves or others, of real apprehension and assent, because we have to secure first the images which are their objects, and these are often peculiar and special. They depend on personal experience; and the experience of one man is not the experience of another. Real assent, then, as the experience which it presupposes, is proper to the individual, and, as such, thwarts rather than promotes the intercourse of man with man. It shuts itself up, as it were, in its own home, or at least it is its own witness and its own standard; and ... it cannot be reckoned on, anticipated, accounted for, inasmuch as it is the accident of this man or that. ... An abstraction can be made at will, and may be the work of a moment; but the moral experiences which perpetuate themselves in images, must be sought after in order to be found, and encouraged and cultivated in order to be appropriated. (*Grammar of Assent*, 309)

"Heart Speaks to Heart"

imagination for Newman is the conscience, which provides the imagination with the perception of divinity.

Newman's concern with how the human person is able to realize the presence of the invisible divine world is one of Newman's most influential spiritual theological ideas. Wilfrid Ward, an influential British theologian writing at the turn of the twentieth century, was highly influenced (and inspired) by Newman's recognition of sanctity as realizing the presence of the divine world within one's conscience. An exploration into Wilfrid Ward's understanding of sanctity helps to highlight the significance of Newman's.

WILFRID WARD'S INTERPRETATION OF NEWMAN'S NOTION OF SANCTITY

Wilfrid Ward (1856–1916), the son of William George Ward (1812–82),[44] greatly admired Newman's spiritual theology, particularly that pertaining to the personal connection between the visible and invisible worlds by virtue of the human conscience and imagination. Ward went so far as to argue that Newman's greatest philosophical achievement, as well as the philosophical and theological center of his thought was encapsulated in Newman's two mottoes: *Cor ad cor loquitur*, translated as "heart speaks unto heart," and *Ex umbris et imaginibus in veritatem*, translated as "from shadows and images unto truth."[45] Quoting an unpublished letter

---

[44] William George Ward was an Oxford Movement convert and contemporary of Newman's. Different from Newman, Ward was a staunch ultramontanist, who interpreted the doctrine of papal infallibility to its extreme, as is evidenced when he famously stated, "I should like a new papal Bull every morning with my Times at breakfast," when asked whether "there is some limit [to papal authority]. You would not wish for new pronouncements every month." Quoted in Wilfrid Philip Ward, *William George Ward and the Catholic Revival* (New York: Longmans, Green & Co., 1912), 14.

[45] After asking, "What, then, is Newman's philosophical teaching? What [is] his distinctive discovery or doctrine? What great thought, what point of view, has he been the first to present—or seen with a new vividness? What is there in his philosophy which corresponds to Idealism in Berkeley, to Empiricism in Locke, to the philosophy of 'common sense' in Reid?" Ward believed that "these mottoes—chosen incidentally—point the way to the really fundamental element of his [Newman's] philosophy." Wilfrid Philip Ward, "Two Mottoes of Cardinal Newman," in *Problems and Persons* (London: Longmans, Green & Co., 1903), 263–4.

by Newman dated 1876,[46] Ward argued that our "direct analyzable knowledge" of one another is only the "shadow," whereas the "belief is in the substance," which is "in the Reality behind it."[47]

Important for understanding Wilfrid Ward's reception of Newman's spiritual theology is his historical context of the Roman Catholic Modernist Crisis. Catholicism at the turn of the twentieth century experienced what Father Cuthbert so aptly described as feelings of "intellectual unrest" and "intellectual discontent."[48] Much of this unrest and discontent was brought about by concern with the "critical inquiry into the subjective conditions of knowing what is true," which, as William L. Portier argues, "is a big part of the intellectual inheritance of theology after Kant."[49] The crux of the

---

[46] I have yet to locate the letter in his *Letters and Diaries* or in his unpublished correspondence housed at the Birmingham Oratory.

[47] Ward, "Two Mottoes of Cardinal Newman," in *Problems and Persons*, 264. The whole quotation is: "He [Newman] wrote some pregnant sentences on the knowledge which one thinking being has of his fellows. 'Our experience of each other, or of society,' he wrote, 'has the two characteristics of conveying to us a knowledge of others, yet bringing home to us our ignorance of them.' Referring to the whole visible world, he says: 'What is my belief in its reality?' In each case—of spirit and of matter—the *direct analyzable knowledge* is but the shadow; the belief is in the substance—in the Reality behind it." Newman is likely contending with the Nativist interpretations of sense perception here. See Edward C. Carterette and Morton P. Friedman, eds., *Handbook of Perception*, vol. I: *Historical and Philosophical Roots of Perception* (New York: Academic Press, 1974), 96–102, for background into the difference between empiricist and nativist understandings of sense perception. Nativism and empiricism are rival epistemologies. Nativism assumes that elements of our understanding of the world are innate to us, meaning that our understanding of the world is part of our human nature. Empiricists, on the other hand, argue that all we know comes from sense perception. Important here is that Newman turns more toward a personalist approach to perceiving the mystery of the other, rather than nativism or a strict empiricism.

[48] Father Cuthbert, O.S.F.C., "Wilfrid Ward," *Dublin Review* 99 (July 1916), 7–9. In his obituary for Wilfrid Ward, Fr. Cuthbert wrote, "Few people outside the Catholic body were aware at the time of intense renewal of thought which was quietly manifesting itself here and there throughout the Catholic world. In all manner of places there was a feeling of intellectual unrest, a calling for a re-statement of theology and philosophy to meet the historical and scientific investigations of the day." Similarly, he wrote, "It is well to note the fact that Wilfrid Ward's advocacy of Newman's theory of development was not merely for the defense of Rome against non-Catholic misunderstandings: he deemed it even more needful for the guidance of that Catholic movement of thought which he hoped would emerge from the intellectual discontent of the movement against Catholics themselves."

[49] William L. Portier, *Divided Friends: Portraits of the Roman Catholic Modernist*

unrest is represented in what Edward Schillebeeckx described as a "problem of the relationship between experience and concept."[50] The Neo-Scholasticism of the late nineteenth and early twentieth centuries, which was also the prevailing orthodoxy, emphasized an "unmediated objectivity" or "conceptualism,"[51] which was countered by the notion that divine revelation is mediated in the experience of human subjects. This divide came to a point when Pope Pius X condemned Modernism in his encyclical *Pascendi Dominici Gregis* (1907) as the "synthesis of all heresies," when he spoke of "sentiment and action as giving rise to 'purely subjective truth.'"[52]

At the heart of the modernist controversies was the question of how human subjects are able to experience the transcendent God, or how are humans living in our material reality able to perceive of the presence of the invisible reality. Many theologians turned to Newman for their exploration of this question. However, the fear of the prevailing Neo-Scholasticism was that their search for the answer to this query led to an overly-interiorized, or overly-subjective spirituality. Pius X's concern, for example, was that the "purely subjective truth," which he saw in what he deemed "Modernism," is "of no use to the man who wants to know above all things whether outside himself there is a God into whose hands he is to one day fall."[53] The Neo-Scholastic response to the post-Kantian turn to the subject was a "massive reassertion of objectivity in the face of the perceived chaos."[54] This reassertion of objectivity, however, left many searching for ways of conceptualizing our relationship with God and our reception of divine revelation outside of what many viewed as a stale intellectualism. The Neo-Scholasticism at the time tended to thematize the intellect in a way that did not allow for a personal way to talk about faith.

Many thinkers of the modernist era, including Wilfrid Ward, found theological solace in the Christian saints (mystics) because

---

Crisis in the United States (Washington, DC: The Catholic University of America Press, 2013), xix.

[50] See Edward Schillebeeckx, O.P., *Revelation and Theology*, trans. N. D. Smith, 2 vols. (New York: Sheed and Ward, 1968), II, 13.

[51] See Portier, *Divided Friends*, xix.

[52] Portier, *Divided Friends*, xviii. The English text of *Pascendi Dominici Gregis* can be found in Claudia Carlen, I.H.M., ed., *The Papal Encyclicals*, 5 vols. (Raleigh, NC: McGrath, 1981), V, 71–97, §39.

[53] Ibid.

[54] See Portier, *Divided Friends*, xix.

they allowed for an avenue to think about the personal experience of Christian faith within the context of Christian voices who were understood as speaking safely from within the borders of Christian doctrine. Ward was interested in how Newman's spirituality could help him explain a theology of sanctity that highlighted the importance of the Christian perception of divine reality (the invisible world) for the vitality of the Church. Ward, however, saw his interpretation of Newman's theology of sanctity as a *via media* between the extremities plaguing the first decade of twentieth-century Catholic theology.

Ward latched onto Newman's notion that to grow in holiness is to become more attuned to divine invisible reality. For both Newman and Ward, what we are able to analyze by means of our senses is not considered as real as the divine reality that lies beyond it. Ward described the conscience in human persons as the basis for how the transcendent God is revealed to us.[55] Ward noted that just as the "mind speaks to mind, and the soul to soul, imperfectly indeed, but by a seemingly direct process," so do we in the visible world correspond, though imperfectly, with the invisible world through faith. For both Newman and Ward, "The Reality as a whole we cannot know. Portions of it flash upon us, we understand not fully how, through the knowledge of its shadow—of the physical signs whereby it expresses itself. We see the visible, we have faith in the invisible."[56]

This philosophical center, as Ward described Newman's theology of the relationship of the invisible reality to our material world, would become the basis of Ward's argument that the saints, whom Ward described as models of sanctity, provide for us an authoritative lens through which to understand our own faith. Ward made this argument throughout his tenure in the Synthetic Society.[57]

---

[55] For the most comprehensive explanation of Newman's personalism, see John F. Crosby, *The Personalism of John Henry Newman* (Washington DC: The Catholic University of America Press, 2014).

[56] Ward, "Two Mottoes of Cardinal Newman," in his *Problems and Persons*, 265–6. On this point, Ward places Newman and Immanuel Kant in conversation, which will be discussed in the section concerning the Synthetic Society in the following chapter.

[57] The Synthetic Society was basically a philosophical think tank made up of English intelligentsia at the turn of the twentieth century that sought to come up with a "working philosophy of religious belief."

"Heart Speaks to Heart"

Central to Ward's argument is the notion that human belief and morality extend from a divine cause or, said another way, that they come from a divine author. "It seems, at least, clear that a 'working philosophy' of religious belief," argued Ward, "cannot leave out of account what has so much influence as a cause of belief, and what has certainly in it at least some rational value attaching to the argument from man's moral nature to a moral author of the universe and of humanity."[58]

Two related questions arose for Ward from this idea that our sense of morality and doctrine are extrinsically linked to a divine cause. The first is, if our religious sense is in fact from God, then *who* do we look to in order to recognize adequately that what we are imagining is really God, who is at the same time transcendent, immanent, and invisible. Related to this first question was also whose faith should be the model for those of us who still see through the glass darkly. The second question was related to our human access to invisible divine realities. Ward sought to answer *how* the saints are able to provide a witness that can—and according to Ward, should be—understood as authoritative for an understanding of the particular religion.[59]

Ward's first question concerning *who* should be viewed as authoritative is related to his question of *how* the saints are authoritative. In the Synthetic Society, Ward was writing in a context in which a person's subjective religious experience was often lauded as authoritative over and against the authority of what he called the "experts," whom, in terms of faith and morals, he collectively labeled "saints." Ward, however, argued that it is better to look to the moral and spiritual experts, as opposed to our own individual minds, which may not be as adequately formed. "For the conquests of the human mind in astronomy," Ward contends, "we look to

---

[58] Wilfrid Ward, "Memorandum" (February 1896), *Papers Read before the Synthetic Society 1895–1908 and Written Comments thereon Circulated among the Members of the Society (for private circulation)* (Printed by Spottiswoode & Co., 1909), 18. (Hereafter, *Synthetic Society Papers*.)

[59] Ward began his argumentation through a more zoomed-out lens that the saints in any religion should tell us about the essence of the religion. However, Ward's more epistemological explanation of how that works in the saints is clearly more interested in particularities and is squarely from within the Christian perspective.

the astronomers"; likewise, "for its conquests in religion we look to the Saints and moral heroes."[60]

Ward, however, qualified his analogy of looking to astronomers for knowledge pertaining to astronomy with the notion that our general knowledge of the mathematical apparatuses behind the astronomer's conclusions is comprehensible by the average person. This in turn is able to lead to confidence in their scientific results. "The individual can (at least in most cases) understand enough of the methods employed by mathematical or astronomical specialists to justify his confidence in their results,"[61] wrote Ward.

Our knowledge of divinity, however, Ward exclaimed, is different because, in the case of religion, "the very nature of the path whereby the moral hero attains the full extent of his confidence in an overruling Deity remains to a large extent shrouded in mystery. He cannot fully explain it even to himself."[62] Because of this, Ward argued, "it belongs to the same category as those intuitions of genius which have not as yet received full analytical interpretation."[63] Ward noted that, even though divine mystery does not allow for knowledge of "ultimate laws connecting phenomena,"[64] there are *real* (empirical) practical imports associated with the imitation of the saints.

Ward recognized that "it is the path of wisdom to be guided by empirical laws while we remain in ignorance of the ultimate laws to which they are resolvable."[65] "Our ancestors guided their ships by the stars though they were ignorant of Copernicanism,"[66] Ward noted. Quoting a maxim of Joubert "In poetry I should fear to be wrong if I differed from the poets, in religion if I differed from the Saints,"[67] Ward sought to explain the relationship between the conscience of the saint and his or her relationship with God and how that relationship works to provide empirical evidence for that which exists beyond human sensory experience.

---

[60] Ward, "Untitled" (May 1896), *Synthetic Society Papers*, 52.
[61] Ibid.
[62] Ibid.
[63] Ibid.
[64] Ibid.
[65] Ibid., 53.
[66] Ibid.
[67] Ibid. This appears to be a paraphrase of some ideas found in Joseph Joubert (1754–1824), a French moralist and essayist whose writings were published posthumously around the time Ward was writing.

"Heart Speaks to Heart"

Ward's explanation as to *how* the saints provide an authoritative witness further explains his question of *whose* experience of the divine should be understood as authoritative. The first hurdle Ward traversed in this question was to argue that what makes the saints distinct is their developed human nature due to their attention and closeness to divinity. Ward identified the question as "how do we justify the statement that Theism is the necessary presupposition of the facts of experience, and especially of ethical experience."[68] He suggested "that this question is best answered by studying the experience of the most highly developed natures."[69] The developed nature of the "saint," Ward argued, more than yielding "a complete account of the grounds for Theism," acts as "an evidence of our personal relations with God, and as supplying what Natural Theology leaves incomplete in its testimony of the moral character of the Deity."[70]

Harkening to Newman as a saint figure himself—and now we can claim with certainty Newman's sainthood!—Ward argued that the moral character of the saint, who has developed his or her character to the point of recognizing its divine origin, is intimately connected with the moral character of God. "Newman's pursuit of the path marked out by conscience at the cost of much suffering," Ward wrote, "brings home to us that there is tragic pathos as well as true poetry in 'Lead, Kindly Light.'"[71] The way Newman was able to follow the "distant and often dim" "divine light" was through "the illative sense," which Ward located as "the automatic action of our rational nature whereby all facts are felt and weighed, and the mind led on to its conclusion from premises of which it is only partially conscious."[72] Or, to be more specific, the illative sense can be understood as akin to Aristotle's notion of *phronesis*.

---

[68] *Ibid.*, 63.

[69] *Ibid.* The month before Ward writes along these lines, "If Kant and Cardinal Newman are right, that the full realization of the significance of the ethical nature is that which gives alike motive and power to rise from suspense to certainty as to the truth of Theism, the *authorities* on the subject are surely those whose ethical nature is most highly developed, and whose religious experience is fullest." "Untitled" (May 1896), *Synthetic Society Papers*, 51.

[70] Ward, "Untitled" (June 1896), *Synthetic Society Papers*, 61.

[71] Ward, *Ten Personal Studies* (London: Longmans, Green & Co., 1908), 229.

[72] *Ibid.*, 230. Ward made no distinction between the conscience and the illative sense.

Ward described that Newman's own "sense of sin, and the presence of God as revealed in conscience, kept unmistakably present for him a divine light for the rays of which he often sought in vain in the world around him."[73] Ward explained that Newman "found the most cogent evidence of God's presence not in the outer world, but in the moral order and the heart of man."[74] Similarly, Newman, Ward argued, was convinced of God's providence within the course for his own life and, therefore, "his search amid the darkness, the 'encircling gloom' of the world, was double—a search for visible tokens of the God of his conscience, and a search for the Light which should define and make clear his own path."[75]

For Ward, the holiness of the saints provides a guide for perceiving God in our worship and devotions. Ward argued that "the accumulated experiences" of the saints provide a definitive testimony of their experience of the divine that can then serve as an objective measure from which to analyze our own subjective spiritual experiences. The collective experience of the saints acts as a compass for our individual, as well as the ecclesial, experience of the unseen divine by means of our religious practice. Our collective and unified prayer within liturgical practice, for example, is how we pray with the saints and experience divinity most fully while in our state of mortality. Similarly, the sensory experience of the liturgy (sounds, smells, tastes, sights, etc.) makes the invisible tangible for worshipers. In moral terms, it is the human conscience that makes the ethical experience of God more tangible to Christians.

Ward noted that while we are unable to understand completely the nature of the divine, we can understand religion, and it is through religion that the saints act as a compass:

> The human race, which is endowed with touch but not with sight of religious truth, which is universally sensitive to the warning touch of an unseen hand in the ethical nature, and is yet unable to descry[76] that region in which the explanation it suggests is verified is surely not acting beyond its competence if it strives, under the guidance of its most sensitive minds to co-ordinate such indications as are given to it of our practical

---

[73] Ibid., 231.
[74] Ibid.
[75] Ibid.
[76] The term "descry" is a verb, which means to catch sight of or to discover.

> relations with realities which, as they are in themselves, are transcendent to our present experience.[77]

For Ward, though we cannot see God, much like the blind cannot see the world, we are still able to navigate transcendent religious experience through the witness of the saints by means of the Church.

Much like we saw in Newman, Ward, though often speaking of the personal nature of religious practice, was deeply invested in the communal, or ecclesial, nature of conscience. Ward argued that "conscience is the point at which human experience touches the borders of the divine, and it supplies a touchstone for testing a revelation which comes from a mind whose direct experience is of Divine Truth."[78] Ward explained that "Christ, who is at once God and Man, supplies the meeting-ground for human experience and divine," and that "the Christian revelation is the fulfilment and further development of the voice in conscience which speaks to us of God and our duty, and is accepted by us as completing its intimations and expressed by the symbols of dogmatic formulae."[79] "Conscience," Ward noted, "though developed in various degrees in individuals, is universal to man."[80]

It is difficult to overstate the importance of the universality and ecclesio-centricity of conscience for Newman's and Ward's contexts. Newman often spoke against the liberalism of his day, which Ward quoted Newman as describing it as

> the doctrine that there is no positive truth in religion, but that one creed is as good as another, and this is the teaching which is gaining substance and force daily. It is inconsistent with any recognition of any religion, as *true*. It teaches that all are to be tolerated, for all are matters of opinion. Revealed religion is not a truth, but a sentiment and a taste; not an objective fact, not miraculous; and it is the right of each individual to make it say just what strikes his fancy. Devotion is not necessarily founded on faith.[81]

---

[77] Ward, "Untitled" (May 7, 1897), *Synthetic Society Papers*, 126.
[78] Wilfrid Ward, *Last Lectures* (London: Longmans, Green & Co., 1918), 101.
[79] Ibid.
[80] Ibid.
[81] Newman, *Biglietto Speech*, quoted in Wilfrid Ward, *The Life of John Henry Cardinal Newman based on his Private Journals and Correspondence* (London: Longmans, Green & Co., 1912), II, 461.

Ward identified with Newman's disdain of liberalism because he experienced many of the same traits expressed by theologians in his own day. The idea of a personal conscience as experiencing divine reality only within the structures of the practices and beliefs of the living *ecclesia* allowed both Newman and Ward to argue for the personal nature of the human reception of divine revelation, while avoiding the traps of liberalism and individualism.

CONCLUSION

To grow in holiness for both Newman and Ward was to perceive the invisible God more fully within our human conscience. Francis Thompson (1859–1907) articulated the spiritual conundrum of sanctity in his poem "The Kingdom of God":

> *O world invisible, we view thee,*
> *O World intangible, we touch thee,*
> *O world unknowable, we know thee,*
> *Inapprehensible, we clutch thee!*[82]

As Christians, we profess in the Nicene Creed to believe in a God who created, "all things visible and invisible." To have faith in the divine is to profess the deeper reality beyond what seems so real to us: our families, our friends, our food, money, the weather, etc. The deeper invisible reality can only be accessed or experienced as one grows in holiness.

To put it simply, to know, experience, and participate in the life of the invisible God is to grow in likeness to God. As one becomes more like or more attuned to the holiness of the divine world, one begins to perceive God's presence within our own world and lives. While the patristic authors so very clearly know this, the rise of empiricism, skepticism, and intellectualism in the last two centuries has at times clouded this understanding of spirituality, creating an environment in which authors such as St. John Henry Newman and Wilfrid Ward were compelled to articulate a way in which we can have certainty that our growth in holiness is in fact a growth toward the Triune God.

---

[82] Francis Thompson, "The Kingdom of God," in *Selected Poems* (London: Burns & Oates, 1909), 189.

"Heart Speaks to Heart"

Found in the portraits of sanctity in both St. Newman and Wilfrid Ward are descriptions of how we, as human beings created in the image of God, are able to recognize by means of the saints and the worship of the Church that we are also growing in likeness to God. In other words, in the writings of these two theologians are explanations—Newman's perhaps more profound that Ward's at times—of how we as humans are able to recognize the presence of the invisible and personal God within our own lives, but also within the traditions of the Church and lives of the saints.

7

Saint John Henry Newman and the Ventures of Faith

Christopher O. Blum

N EAR THE BEGINNING of Jane Austen's *Mansfield Park*, we meet Edmund Bertram, an aspirant to Anglican orders in the early years of the nineteenth century. Edmund will eventually be ordained and, by the time we have finished the story, we are confident that he will be a dutiful country parson. Yet, when we first learn of his religious convictions, we are not sure that his faith will withstand the lure of the world, represented by the charming and intelligent Mary Crawford. While she and Edmund tour the chapel of a venerable mansion, Mary allows an expression of disdain for religious observance to escape her lips: "Cannot you imagine with what unwilling feelings the former belles of the house of Rushworth did many a time repair to this chapel?" Edmund's response to her railery was ultimately insufficient because sentimental: "I have not yet left Oxford long enough to forget what chapel prayers are."[1] With this example in mind, we can appreciate that John Henry Newman should have found Austen's clergymen wanting: "What vile creatures her parsons are! she has not a dream of the high Catholic."[2] What was it that

---

[1] Jane Austen, *Mansfield Park*, ed. James Kinsley (Oxford: Oxford University Press, 1980), 69.
[2] Quoted in Ian Ker, *John Henry Newman: A Biography* (Oxford: Oxford University Press, 1988), 138. Newman had been reading *Emma*, and so that negative judgment seems likely to have been elicited by her character the Revered Philip Elton. Yet, as it was cast in universal terms, it may be taken as a general judgment upon all her clerical characters.

Edmund Bertram lacked? "Let those who take pleasure in religious worship," Newman exhorted his Oxford parishioners in 1831, "aim at inward sanctity."[3] The advice would have been helpful to Austen's hero, whose shortcoming was that he lacked the "high and unearthly spirit" of faith that Newman took it as his task to inspire in those who heard his sermons.[4]

Among Newman's sermons, one has long stood out as an exhortation to an active and life-changing belief in Christ: "The Ventures of Faith." We will here approach that sermon by first recalling that Newman took faith to have as its object divine truth expressed in "a definite Creed," as he put it in his *Apologia pro Vita Sua*;[5] or, as he affirmed in *The Idea of a University*, that faith is "an intellectual act, its object truth, and its result knowledge."[6] This conviction consistently shaped his contributions to the Oxford Movement, which were spurred by what he called the "vital question": "how were we to keep the Church from being liberalized?"[7] By liberalism, of course, he meant "the anti-dogmatic principle," the denial that the Christian faith's truth-claims about God and man were timeless and binding.[8] After the Reform Bill of 1832, the English parliament included non-conforming Protestants and Irish Roman Catholics. Newman and his friends, therefore, were troubled by the prospect of the Church-by-law-established having its bishops chosen by those who did not belong to it.

It is remarkable that the Oxford Movement was not chiefly a protest or a work of ecclesiastical politics. It was, instead, a genuine search for the renewal of Christian life and holiness. That it should have taken that inspiring form was in large part thanks to Newman. One of the best accounts of the spirit of the Oxford Movement was penned by one of its younger members, Richard Church, who

---

[3] John Henry Newman, "Christian Nobleness," in *Sermons Bearing on Subjects of the Day* (London: Longmans, 1898), 141.

[4] John Henry Newman, "The Ventures of Faith," in *Parochial and Plain Sermons* (London: Longmans, 1919), IV, sermon 10, 295–306, at 306 (hereafter *PPS*). All subsequent quotations from "The Ventures of Faith" will be from this edition.

[5] John Henry Newman, *Apologia pro Vita Sua*, ed. Ian Ker (London: Penguin, 1994), 25.

[6] John Henry Newman, *The Idea of a University* (Tacoma, WA: Cluny Media, 2016), 33.

[7] Newman, *Apologia*, ed. Ker, 46.

[8] See Newman's "Note A" on Liberalism, in *Apologia*, ed. Ker, 252.

remained a life-long Anglican, but nevertheless revered Newman and wrote of him with sympathy and insight. "The movement," Church explained, was

> above all, a moral one ... Its ethical tendency was shown in ... the increased care of the Gospels, and study of them, compared with other parts of the Bible. Evangelical theology had ... regarded the Epistles of St. Paul as the last word of the Gospel message ... The movement made a great change. The great Name stood no longer for an abstract symbol of doctrine, but for a living Master, who could teach as well as save. And not forgetting whither He had gone and what He was, the readers of Scripture now sought Him eagerly in those sacred records, where we can almost see and hear His going in and out among men. It was a change in the look and use of Scripture, which some can still look back to as an epoch in their religious history.[9]

It is precisely this living contact with Jesus, met afresh in the pages of the Gospels, that we see in Newman's sermons.

Before turning to "The Ventures of Faith" as an example of Newman's preaching on faith, we will make a closer approach to its setting. It was preached at a turning point both for the Oxford Movement and for Newman himself. The novelist Anthony Trollope will set the stage for us: "When . . . Dr Whately was made an archbishop, and Dr Hampden some years afterwards Regius professor, many wise divines saw that a change was taking place in men's minds, and that more liberal ideas would henceforward be suitable to the priests as well as to the laity."[10] From the vantage point offered by the year 1857, when those lines were published in Trollope's *Barchester Towers*, it was plain that the appointment of Renn Dickson Hampden as Regius Professor of Divinity in 1836 was the beginning of open conflict at Oxford between the liberals on the one hand, and Newman and his friends, the Tractarians, on the other. Hampden was the very incarnation of the anti-dogmatic principle, and Newman himself went so far as to say that Hampden's teaching would "make shipwreck of Christian faith."[11]

---

[9] R. W. Church, *The Oxford Movement: Twelve Years, 1833–1845*, ed. Geoffrey Best (Chicago: University of Chicago Press, 1970), 133–4.

[10] Anthony Trollope, *Barchester Towers*, ed. John Bowen (1857; Oxford: Oxford University Press, 2014), 18.

[11] In a letter to Hampden, as reported by Newman in *Apologia*, ed. Ker, 68. This is a variant of the same letter as reported in other sources. See, for instance,

"Heart Speaks to Heart"

Hearing of the appointment, Newman and some of his friends met on February 10, 1836 to organize the opposition; one of its features was a pamphlet against Hampden's theology that Newman wrote that very night. On February 20, the day before he preached "The Ventures of Faith," Newman learned that his closest friend, Hurrell Froude, was at last dying of the tuberculosis from which he had been suffering. Froude was by temperament a more active and determined man than his friend. His death would mean a choice for Newman: to step forward into leadership of the movement or to recede into the comparative quiet of his theological studies and pastoral work. The next day, February 21, was Newman's thirty-fifth birthday. The letter he wrote to his sister that day gives us a privileged view into his innermost thoughts at that crossroads in his life:

> Many thanks for the news contained in your letter ... Thank also my Mother and Harriett for their congratulations upon this day. They will be deserved if God gives me grace to fulfil the purposes for which He has led me on hitherto in a wonderful way. I think I am conscious to myself that, whatever are my faults, I wish to live and die to His glory—to surrender wholly to Him as His instrument, to whatever work and at whatever personal sacrifice, though I cannot duly realize my own words when I say so. He is teaching me, it would seem, to depend on Him only; for, as perhaps Rogers told you, I am soon to lose dear Froude—which, looking forward to the next twenty-five years of my life, and its probable occupations, is the greatest loss I could have.[12]

This confession is not only a testimony to Newman's deep personal attachment to the will of God; it was, as we shall see, a meditation parallel to the sermon he preached that afternoon: "The Ventures of Faith."

As with any good Catholic sermon today, Newman's were rooted in the Gospel texts proposed by the liturgical calendar. For that Sunday in 1836, he was offered St. Mark's version of the episode of James's and John's request to sit at the Lord's right and left (Mk

---

Marvin R. O'Connell, *The Oxford Conspirators: A History of the Oxford Movement 1833–45* (New York, 1969), 181.

[12] Letter of John Henry Newman to his sister Jemima, February 21, 1836, available here: http://www.newmanreader.org/biography/mozley/volume2/file6.html.

10:35–45). It would have been conventional to consider the request as an instance of the disciples' imperfect understanding of Jesus' teaching and mission and to have criticized James and John for their disordered desire for power and rank. Instead, Newman turned his attention to the generosity of their response to Jesus' question, "Are you able to drink the cup that I drink, or to be baptized with the baptism with which I am baptized?" (Mk 10:38) Let us listen to the sermon's opening paragraph:

> "They said to Him, we are able." These words of the holy Apostles James and John were in reply to a very solemn question addressed to them by their Divine Master. They coveted, with a noble ambition, though as yet unpracticed in the highest wisdom, untaught in the holiest truth—they coveted to sit beside Him on His Throne of Glory. They would be content with nothing short of that special gift which He had come to grant to His elect, which He shortly after died to purchase for them, and which He offers to us. They ask the gift of eternal life; and He in answer told them, not that they should have it (though for them it was really reserved), but He reminded them what they must venture for it; "Are ye able to drink of the cup that I shall drink of and to be baptized with the baptism that I am baptized with? They say unto Him, we are able" (Mk 10:38–9). Here then a great lesson is impressed upon us, that our duty as Christians lies in this, in making ventures for eternal life without the absolute certainty of success.[13]

Newman's thesis is a claim about what he called "the excellence and nobleness of faith": namely, that "its presence implies that we have the heart to make a venture."[14]

The ensuing sermon may be divided into three parts. In the first, Newman proved the accuracy of his account of faith. In the second, he posed and then responded to a significant objection: that Christians do not seem to live up to this account of faith. In the final part, he showed how God honors and accepts the ventures of faith that we do make. Let us consider the steps of his argument in order.

The contention of "The Ventures of Faith" is that Christian faith is a "making present what is unseen" and, consequently, an "acting upon the mere prospect of it, as if it were really possessed; the

---

[13] Newman, "The Ventures of Faith," 295–6.
[14] *Ibid.*, 296.

venturing upon it, the staking present ease, happiness, or other good, upon the chance of the future":[15] that is, eternal life. How is such a conception of faith to be sustained? The argument is a theological one, and so consisted in the sayings and deeds recorded in Sacred Scripture. Newman proceeded by way of induction, piling up instance after instance so as to convince the hearer that he had rightly captured the universal nature of the theological virtue of faith. His evidence included the teaching of St. Paul from Hebrews 11, the example of Abraham leaving his home for a promised land he knew not where, the example at hand of James and John, and, especially, the lesson implied in Jesus' command to St. Peter, "Follow me" (Jn 21:19 and repeated in Jn 21:21). These episodes all show the person or persons summoned by God responding with a "venture," that is, a sacrifice or risk. "We give up our all to Him," as Newman put it, "and He is to claim this or that ... according to His good pleasure." He then brought the first part of his sermon to a close with an elegant demonstration: "If then faith be the essence of a Christian life, and if it be what I have now described, it follows that our duty lies in risking upon Christ's word what we have, for what we have not; and doing so in a noble, generous way."[16]

The evident objection to this account is that ordinary Christians do not seem to embrace it, and yet ordinary Christians must be presumed to have faith. Newman wanted his hearers to feel the full force of this objection and to apply it to themselves. "Let everyone who hears me ask himself the question, what stake has he in the truth of Christ's promise? How would he be a whit the worse-off, supposing (which is impossible), but supposing it to fail?"[17] He pressed this question on his audience: "What have we ventured for Christ?"[18] And he insisted that they ask just what their risky investment in the Gospel had been to date. He left them wondering and worrying whether their religion was anything more noble than conformity with the expectations of polite society.

Yet, he would not leave his congregation despondent; nor was there even a hint of irony in his sermon. He raised the question in order to make his hearers the more sensible of the kind of acts of

---

[15] Ibid., 297.
[16] Ibid., 299.
[17] Ibid., 300.
[18] Ibid., 301.

faith (and, we may be inclined to add, of hope and of charity) that good Christians have always embraced. He turned to examples: almsgiving, the sacrifice of wealth or power "in order to be nearer Christ," the setting aside of comfort in favor of the performance of godly duty, repentance of sin and the choice to amend one's life, and the heartfelt "Thy will be done" prayed while suffering. These are the ordinary and everyday ventures of faith. By enumerating them, Newman restored the confidence of his flock. They were now ready to hear the final part of his message.

The person who makes any such ventures, or still greater ones, is "taken at his word, while he understands not, perhaps, what he says; but he is accepted, as meaning somewhat and risking much."[19] Newman praised the "generous hearts" of James and John, and then the generous hearts of all those who willingly make a vow of service, as at Confirmation or the reception of Holy Orders, and, we may add, Holy Matrimony. Such ventures are the turning points of any Christian life:

> in various ways, the circumstances of the times cause men at certain seasons to take this path or that, for religion's sake. They know not whither they are being carried; they see not the end of their course; they know no more than this, that it is right to do what they are now doing; and they hear a whisper within them, which assures them, as it did the two holy brothers, that whatever their present conduct involves in time to come, they shall, through God's grace, be equal to it.[20]

This was a most stirring invitation to radical Christian commitment, be it in the married estate or consecrated life. It was a call to mission, and we can suppose that Newman wrote those words feelingly, given what he was experiencing during the days leading up to the delivery of the sermon.

"The Ventures of Faith" came to a fitting end. Having evoked the bloody martyrdom of St. James and the long, drawn-out, white martyrdom of St. John, Newman closed with a direct exhortation:

> Alas! that we, my brethren, have not more of this high and unearthly spirit! How is it that we are so contented with things as they are—that we are so willing to be let alone, and to enjoy this life—that we make such excuses, if any one presses on us

---

[19] Ibid., 304.
[20] Ibid., 304–5.

the necessity of something higher, the duty of bearing the Cross, if we would earn the Crown, of the Lord Jesus Christ? I repeat it; what are our ventures and risks upon the truth of His word? for He says expressly, "Everyone who has forsaken houses, or brothers or sisters, or father, or mother, or wife, or children, or lands, for My Name's sake, shall receive a hundred-fold, and shall inherit everlasting life" (Mt 19:29).[21]

It was a beautiful example of Newman at his best as a preacher: full of sympathy, but also incisive and challenging. His sermons focused on Christ and his offer of salvation, but were also attentive to the rhythms and cares of our lives. "The Ventures of Faith" is just as inspiring and applicable today as it was in 1836.

For Newman himself, he would later describe the five years that followed the delivery of this sermon as the happiest of his life—with the important qualification: "in a human point of view."[22] During those years, he was extraordinarily productive: writing tracts, historical sketches, and theological essays, editing multiple books as well as a theological journal, and all the while continuing to preach at St. Mary's. But soon he would no longer be "at home," as he put it.[23] The witness of the early centuries of the Church coupled with the sinuous course of Anglican theological debates would lead him to recognize that it was the Church of Rome and not of Canterbury and London that was the Church of the Fathers. Truly, his leading role in the Oxford Movement was for John Henry Newman a great "venture of faith," the final result of which he could not see, for what it led him to was the Catholic priesthood and, now in our days, to our altars as a canonized saint.

"The Ventures of Faith" was a small masterpiece of the oratorical art, but it was no less characteristic of Newman's preaching for having been so finely wrought or deeply moving. The sermons that he preached from the pulpit of St. Mary's between 1828 and 1841 have been often republished and treasured by readers for generations. During the Oxford Movement, their influence on the minds of his students, most of them candidates for Anglican orders, was incalculable. One frequent auditor said this of them: "He reached the heart of young Oxford; man after man, in whom was the recep-

---

[21] Ibid., 306.
[22] Newman, *Apologia*, ed. Ker, 82.
[23] Ibid.

tive faculty, received the living force of his words and reproduced so far as he was able the Master's spirit in himself."[24] What they received was not, however, chiefly Newman's personality. Richard Church, who also heard the sermons, said that they communicated Newman's "absolute and burning faith in God and His counsels [and] in His love," but added, crucially, that the sermons "made men think of the things which the preacher spoke of, and not of the sermon or of the preacher."[25] And that is the truest and best praise any speaker could receive.

Newman's sermons are suffused with an ardent devotion to Jesus Christ. The most eminent student of his writings in our day—Father Ian Ker—explained using Newman's own words that his aim had been "to present the person of Christ not in an 'unreal way—as a mere idea or vision,' but as 'Scripture has set Him before us in His actual sojourn on earth, in His gestures, words, and deeds.'"[26] For us, perhaps the greatest lesson that we can take from Newman is the encouragement to stay close to Christ in the pages of the Gospels, which he called "the best book of meditations which can be, because it is divine."[27] By regularly reading the Gospels, we can build up in ourselves that "intimate, immediate dependence on Emmanuel, God with us," that Newman called "almost the definition of a Christian."[28]

---

[24] Samuel Wilberforce, quoted in O'Connell, *Oxford Conspirators*, 215–16.
[25] Church, *Oxford Movement*, 93.
[26] Ker, *John Henry Newman*, 100, quoting John Henry Newman, "The Tears of Christ at the Grave of Lazarus," in *PPS*, III, sermon 10, 130–1.
[27] Quoted in Ker, *John Henry Newman*, 671.
[28] John Henry Newman, "Waiting for Christ," as presented in John Henry Newman, *Waiting for Christ: Meditations for Advent and Christmas*, ed. Christopher O. Blum (Greenwood Village, CO: Augustine Institute, 2018), 20.

8

"Until Christ be Formed in You"[1]

Saint John Henry Newman's
Theological-Pastoral Mystagogy

Robert P. Imbelli

INTRODUCTION

I BEGIN WITH SOME BRIEF REMARKS about the title of the essay itself, since it already sums up the thrust of these reflections. By employing the term "mystagogy," literally a leading into the Mystery, I raise up Newman's profound sense of God's Mystery, God's holiness and otherness from all finite, created reality.

This intense sense of God's Holy Mystery impressed itself upon Newman from an early age and it evoked from him throughout his life sentiments of awe, reverence, and wonder. His worshipful response finds apt expression in the words of one of his best-loved poem/hymns: "Praise to the Holiest in the Height, and in the depth be praise. In all his words most wonderful, most sure in all his ways."

Newman's foundational sense of God's Mystery, like a diamond, is brilliantly reflected in three facets. First, he (and we) confess and meditate upon the Mystery. This is the theological facet. Second, the Mystery must be lived and we must conform our lives to its exigencies: the facet of spirituality. Third, the good news of the Mystery must be communicated and shared: the pastoral-ministerial facet.

In Newman's life, these three facets of his encounter with God's Holy Mystery are inseparable and indispensable. This is one of the

---

[1] Gal. 4:19.

prime reasons that he is so exemplary a figure: indeed, a providential saint and teacher for our times. He refuses to countenance any divorce of spirituality, theology, and pastoral ministry, but sees them as constituting a complex and vivifying whole.[2]

A final preliminary point: "Mystery" in Catholic theology does not indicate a puzzle or enigma, an absence of light. Rather, it signifies a superabundance of Light. And even in the gracious revelation of God's holy Mystery, it remains inexhaustible. Indeed, God's supreme revelation in the crucified, risen, and ascended Jesus Christ does not lessen the Mystery, but only deepens it.

Thus, even as we, like Newman, seek to realize something of God's Glory revealed in Jesus Christ, even as we confess, meditate, live and teach this saving Mystery, we are constantly drawn back to the foundational doxological imperative of praise: "Praise to the Holiest in the Height, and in the depth be praise. In all his words most wonderful, most sure in all his ways!"

THE MIND OF NEWMAN

One of the distinguishing characteristics of John Henry Newman, making him a particularly apt intellectual and spiritual teacher for our time, is the capaciously Catholic breadth of his intellect. He embodies in his person a comprehensiveness of outlook that resists partial views of reality. His is the quintessentially Catholic affirmation of "both/and."

Unlike the narrow rationalists of his own day and ours, Newman's is not a constricted view of reason, but one that recognizes legitimate cognitive insights in non-scientific domains, like music and poetry. Indeed, he himself was accomplished in both areas.[3] Like the Fathers of the Church whom he so loved, Newman did not divorce mind and heart in the journey to God. His integral vision embraced both and saw that the scientific, the moral, and the aesthetic together comprise an integral anthropology. Ignoring or denying any dimension produces a truncated understanding of the

---

[2] Louis Bouyer is a sure guide in exploring Newman's holistic vision. See Louis Bouyer, *Newman's Vision of Faith: A Theology for a Time of General Apostasy* (San Francisco: Ignatius Press, 1986).

[3] The indispensable study in this regard is Guy Nicholls, *Unearthly Beauty: The Aesthetic of St John Henry Newman* (Leominster: Gracewing, 2019).

human, harmful not only to the individual, but to the community and, ultimately, to nature itself.[4]

A key feature of Newman's integral anthropology is the importance he assigns to the imagination. Somewhat surprisingly, "Newman did not set out a definition of the 'imagination.'"[5] Rather, he associated this capacity of the mind with the concrete apprehension and appropriation of reality, in particular in the realm of the interpersonal and the affective. In a famous observation, he asserts, "The heart is commonly reached, not through the reason, but through the imagination, by means of direct impressions, by the testimony of facts and events, by history, by description. Persons influence us, voices melt us, looks subdue us, deeds inflame us."[6]

Thus, in speaking of the "mind" of Newman, one must not exclude the "heart" as the seat of affections and imagination. It is both significant and indicative that Newman chose as his cardinalatial motto *Cor ad cor loquitur*—"Heart speaks to heart." Unlike the great philosophers of modernity, represented by Descartes and Kant, who focus upon the individual almost in autonomous isolation from others, Newman's whole intellectual disposition is intrinsically interpersonal. In many respects, he anticipated the personalist vision of a Martin Buber and Gabriel Marcel.[7] Commenting on this aspect of Newman's thought and sensibility, Nicholas Lash writes: "The mode of rationality appropriate to such apprehension is—in its concreteness and irreducible complexity—closer to 'personal knowledge' or to literary and aesthetic cognition, than it is to the 'linear' rationality characteristic of theoretical deduction."[8]

---

[4] Notice the close link Pope Francis draws between an integral anthropology and ecology in his encyclical letter, *Laudato Sí: On Care for Our Common Home*, ch. 3: "The Human Roots of the Ecological Crisis."

[5] Bernard Dive, *John Henry Newman and the Imagination* (London: T. & T. Clark, 2018), 14.

[6] John Henry Newman, *An Essay in Aid of a Grammar of Assent*, edited with Introduction and Notes, I. T. Ker (Oxford: Clarendon Press, 1985), 65–6 (hereafter *Grammar of Assent*).

[7] An important study in this regard is John F. Crosby, *The Personalism of John Henry Newman* (Washington, DC: Catholic University of America Press, 2014).

[8] Nicholas Lash, "Introduction" to John Henry Newman, *An Essay in Aid of a Grammar of Assent* (Notre Dame: University of Notre Dame Press, 1979), 10.

"Heart Speaks to Heart"

A CRUCIAL DISTINCTION: "NOTIONAL" AND "REAL"

In this regard, one of the most characteristic and familiar of Newman's views is the distinction he makes between the "notional" and the "real." He employs it not only in his more technical writings like *The Grammar of Assent*, but it appears prominently in his sermons as he urges his hearers to "realize," to appropriate personally their sacred privileges. In shorthand fashion, one might consider it the distinction between knowledge of the head and knowledge of the heart. One recalls Pascal's famous dictum: "The heart has its reasons which reason does not comprehend" (*Pensées*, no. 423).

Yet, as has already been stressed, it is not a question of either/or, as though only the latter were important and the former otiose. Rather, both are required for a comprehensive understanding. However, in matters religious, the ultimate pastoral aim is not merely notional, but real apprehension and appropriation. Nicholas Lash elucidates further: "This latter way of knowing: engaged, experiential, pre-reflexive, is—and the concept is central to the argument of the *Grammar*—'imaginative.'"[9]

Newman applies the notional/real distinction (not separation!) to the relation between "religion" and "theology." In a typically balanced and challenging statement, he asserts,

> A dogma is a proposition ... To give a real assent to it is an act of religion; to give a notional, is a theological act. It is discerned, rested in, and appropriated as a reality, by the religious imagination; it is held as a truth by the theological intellect. Not as if there were in fact, or could be, any line of demarcation or party-wall between these two modes of assent, the religious and the theological. As intellect is common to all men as well as imagination, every religious man is to a certain extent a theologian, and no theology can start or thrive without the initiative and abiding presence of religion. [Still] ... there is a theological habit of mind, and a religious, each distinct from each, religion using theology, and theology using religion.[10]

Whether in homilies, catechesis, or theological education, the context and audience-appropriate union of the two modes of apprehension is imperative, lest the preacher and teacher succumb either to an arid intellectualism or a flaccid emotionalism.

---

[9] Ibid., 13.
[10] *Grammar of Assent*, 69.

"Until Christ be Formed in You"

INCARNATION: THE CENTRAL IDEA AND IMAGE OF REVELATION

In his *Oxford University Sermons*, which explore at length the relation of faith and reason, Newman insists: "It is the Incarnation of the Son of God rather than any doctrine drawn from a partial view of Scripture (however true and momentous it may be) which is the article of a standing or a falling Church."[11]

Once more, his holistic, synoptic vision perceives that the true *novum* of the New Testament is Jesus Christ himself. As he insisted at the end of his *Lectures on Justification* (perhaps his most systematic work), "The true preaching of the Gospel is to preach Christ."[12] Roderick Strange has highlighted this defining dimension of Newman's faith and thought: "From the doctrine of creation to the doctrine of eschatology, the Christ was central for Newman. Any future study of his theology will be obliged to take this fact into account."[13] As will future studies of Newman's preaching.

A helpful beginning is Denis Robinson's study of Newman's sermons. He underscores the inseparability of Newman's theology and his pastoral practice: both are pervasively Christocentric. Robinson writes:

> Newman employs all the devices of homiletic rhetoric at his disposal to encourage his listeners to "realize" the central principle of Christianity, namely, the truth of the Word made Flesh. In Newman's vocabulary, the verb "to realize" is almost a technical term denoting a personal grasp of the reality of a particular object or truth, a grasp so profound that it can move the believer to action.[14]

Related to the Incarnation as the central principle of Christianity is Newman's famous contention, "From the age of fifteen, dogma

---

[11] John Henry Newman, *Oxford University Sermons* (New York: Scribner, 1872), sermon 2, 35. The quotation is from the key second sermon: "The Influence of Natural and Revealed Religion Respectively."

[12] John Henry Newman, *Lectures on the Doctrine of Justification* (London: Longmans & Green, 1914), 325.

[13] Roderick Strange, *Newman and the Gospel of Christ* (Oxford University Press, 1981), 164. Strange has further explored the central place of Christology in *Newman: The Heart of Holiness* (London: Hodder & Stoughton, 2019), 41–9.

[14] Denis Robinson, "Preaching," in Ian Ker and Terrence Merrigan, eds., *The Cambridge Companion to John Henry Newman* (Cambridge: Cambridge University Press, 2009), 241–54, at 248.

has been the fundamental principle of my religion; I know no other religion; I cannot enter into the idea of any other sort of religion; religion, as a mere sentiment is to me a dream and a mockery."[15] And, tellingly, he insists: "my battle was with liberalism; by liberalism I mean the anti-dogmatic principle and its developments."[16]

Newman amplified these terse remarks in his well-known "*Biglietto* Address," delivered in Rome on May 12, 1879, on the occasion of being officially informed of his being raised to the office of cardinal by Pope Leo XIII. Newman spoke these heartfelt words:

> For thirty, forty, fifty years I have resisted to the best of my powers the spirit of liberalism in religion ... Liberalism in religion is the doctrine that there is no positive truth in religion, but that one creed is as good as another, and this is the teaching which is gaining substance and force daily. It is inconsistent with any recognition of any religion, as true. It teaches that all are to be tolerated, for all are matters of opinion. Revealed religion is not a truth, but a sentiment and a taste; not an objective fact, not miraculous; and it is the right of each individual to make it say just what strikes his fancy. Devotion is not necessarily founded on faith.[17]

One can only marvel at the acuteness and foresight of these words, anticipating the widespread present-day boast of being "spiritual, but not religious."

The "dogmatic principle" is the claim that there is indeed positive truth in religion, and that at the heart of Christianity stands the definitive truth of God's Incarnation in Jesus Christ. But what distinguishes Christianity is the confession that the "dogma" is no abstract principle, but the very Person of Jesus Christ.

Thus, commenting on his use of the term "Idea," Keith Beaumont makes this crucial clarification:

> When Newman speaks of the living "idea" of Christianity, he is referring not just to the *thought* of Christ present in men's minds (though it is doubtless on account of this that he uses the term "idea"), but also, and above all, to the very *Person* of Christ living both in the hearts of individual Christians and in

---

[15] John Henry Newman, *Apologia pro Vita Sua* (London: Longmans & Green, 1913), 49.
[16] Ibid., 48.
[17] John Henry Newman, *Spiritual Writings*, selected with an introduction by John T. Ford (Maryknoll, NY: Orbis Books, 2012), 222.

the whole liturgical and sacramental life of the Church—the Church itself being both "sacrament" and "mystical body" of Christ, and thereby a vehicle of divine Grace.[18]

The remainder of this essay will bring into prominent relief what Cyril O'Regan calls the "Christological contexting" of the Mystery.[19] In so doing, I will seek to show how "Christologically saturated" is Newman's spiritual-pastoral theology. Here again, he appears a much-needed saint and teacher for our time, too often marked and marred by "Christological forgetfulness and deficiency."[20]

THE PRESENCE OF CHRIST IN THE WORLD

In the Letter to the Romans, St. Paul teaches that "When Gentiles who do not have the law do by nature what the law demands, even though they do not have the law, they are a law for themselves. They show that what the law requires is written on their hearts, to which their conscience bears witness" (Rom 2:14–15a). Here, *in nuce*, I suggest, we find Newman's carefully pondered reflections about "natural religion." He considered the subject at length in his early *Oxford University Sermons* and returned to the theme in the *Grammar of Assent*. In both instances, he compared and contrasted "natural religion" with "revealed religion"—as Paul himself had implicitly done.

Newman holds that natural religion is a manifestation of God's providential dispensation for humanity, especially evident in the phenomenon of conscience. In the second of his *Oxford University Sermons*, he writes: "Conscience implies a relation between the soul and a something exterior, and that, moreover, superior to itself; a relation to an excellence which it does not possess, and to a tribunal over which it has no power." He goes further and postulates that "the presentiment of a future life, and of a judgment to be passed upon present conduct, with rewards and punishments

---

[18] Keith Beaumont, *Blessed John Henry Newman: Theologian and Spiritual Guide for Our Times* (San Francisco: Ignatius Press, 2010), 49.

[19] Cyril O'Regan, "Newman and von Balthasar: The Christological Contexting of the Numinous," *Église et théologie* 26 (1995), 165–202.

[20] See Robert P. Imbelli, *Rekindling the Christic Imagination* (Collegeville, MN: Liturgical Press, 2014), xiii–xxviii; and more recently "No Decapitated Body: Remembering and Misremembering Vatican II," *Nova et Vetera* (to appear).

annexed, forms an article, more or less distinct, in the creed of Natural Religion."[21]

Conscience intimates the reality of a Lawgiver, even sounding the echo of a voice. So far "Natural Religion" ventures, yet offers "little or no information respecting what may be called His *Personality*."[22] In a footnote affixed to this passage in the third edition of the volume, however, Newman avers that this claim is "too strongly said." And in the *Grammar of Assent*, he contends that "if, as is the case, we feel responsibility, are ashamed, are frightened, at transgressing the voice of conscience, this implies that there is One to whom we are responsible, before whom we are ashamed, whose claims upon us we fear."[23]

Nonetheless, he admits that when we consider "the course of human affairs," when we ponder the horrors of human history, "what strikes the mind so forcibly and so painfully is [God's] absence (if I may so speak) from His own world." Thus, "my burdened conscience … pronounces without any misgiving that God exists:—and it pronounces quite as surely that I am alienated from Him."[24]

Hence, perhaps the most significant deliverance of Natural Religion is the recognition of its neediness and incapacity, and its anticipation of a remedy for its ills. Newman writes: "Natural Religion is based upon the sense of sin; but it cannot find, it does but look out for the remedy." And he declares: "That remedy, both for guilt and for moral impotence, is found in the central doctrine of Revelation, the Mediation of Christ."[25]

Thus, Natural Religion yearns, however inchoately, for a saving presence that can only be fulfilled in Christ "in whom all the Providences of God centre."[26] And the Gospels, with their inspired depiction of the Image of the Savior, "contain a manifestation of the Divine Nature, so special, as to make it appear from the contrast as if nothing were known of God, when they are unknown."[27]

As Newman hymned in his poem, "Praise to the Holiest,"

---

[21] *Oxford University Sermons*, sermon 2, 18–19 (italics in original).
[22] Ibid., 22.
[23] *Grammar of Assent*, 76.
[24] Ibid., 256.
[25] Ibid., 313.
[26] Ibid., 43.
[27] Ibid., 81.

"Until Christ be Formed in You"

> *And that a higher gift than grace*
> *should flesh and blood refine:*
> *God's Presence and His very self,*
> *And Essence all-divine.*

Moreover, this Incarnation does not serve merely as remedy for sin. It truly recapitulates all those intimations of grace in the lives of individuals and communities. In a passage redolent of his beloved Fathers of the Church, Newman exults:

> Christ came for this very purpose, to gather together in one all the elements of good dispersed throughout the world, to make them his own, to illuminate them with Himself, to reform and refashion them into Himself. He came to make a new and better beginning of all things than Adam had been, and to be a fountain-head from which all good henceforth might flow.[28]

But until Jesus Christ at last appears, these elements remain mere prefigurations at best, but hints and guesses.

THE PRESENCE OF CHRIST IN THE BELIEVER AND IN THE CHURCH

Jesus Christ, the New Adam, in his person is that "fountain-head from which all good might flow." His grace is present and experienced in a surpassing way in the Church in which the Idea or Image (Newman often uses the two interchangeably) of Jesus Christ is shared and nourished. As Terrence Merrigan writes,

> Christianity, for Newman, is not the mere perfection of humanity's natural religious instincts, though it does involve the perfection of all the authentic elements of natural religion. It is a revelation of God that would be unthinkable were it not already realized in the person of Jesus and re-presented in the Church by means of certain sacramental extensions of the Incarnation.[29]

The apostolic preaching, the Gospel narratives, the Church's Tradition, and sacraments convey the idea or image to the believer. But it is clear from Newman's sermons and writings that the believer's faith, though mediated by idea and image, does not

---

[28] *Lectures on the Doctrine of Justification*, 193.
[29] Terrence Merrigan, "Revelation," in *The Cambridge Companion to John Henry Newman*, 47–72, at 55.

rest there. Through them, believers encounter the living Jesus Christ himself whom their hearts so ardently desire. In a remarkable outpouring, Newman rhapsodizes that "the divinely-enlightened mind sees in Christ the very Object whom it desires to love and worship,—the Object correlative of its own affections; and it trusts Him, or believes, from loving Him."[30] Thus, Terrence Merrigan rightly insists, "[T]he dynamism and organizing power of the Christian idea is born of its foundation in the risen Christ, God's living Word in history ... He is the ground, the source of coherence, and the continuing dynamic, of Christian life and reflection, in and through which He is now known and apprehended."[31]

Complimentary to and in intimate connection with "the dogmatic principle," then, is "the sacramental principle." Newman writes in the *Apologia*, "I was confident in the truth of a certain definite religious teaching, based upon this foundation of dogma; viz. that there was a visible Church, with sacraments and rites which are the channels of invisible grace."[32] As embodied creatures, our only access to the spiritual realm is through sacramental embodiment. As Louis Bouyer writes, for Newman "this sacramental world is dominated by that mysterious presence of God in Christ, here and now already, on earth, which is not only a preparation for heaven but its anticipation."[33] And, though to my knowledge he does not use the term, I think it quite congruent with Newman's Christological vision to say that, by his Incarnation, Jesus Christ is himself the "Ur-Sacrament": the font from whom all spiritual blessings flow.

Through Baptism and Eucharist, the Christian "puts on Christ" and is continually nourished by him. The Christian's "justification" consists in far more than a merely extrinsic imputation of righteousness. Through the sacraments, he or she becomes truly conformed to Christ and embarks on the ongoing journey of transformation in Christ. Such is the burden of Newman's *Lectures on Justification*. In Lecture Eight, "Righteousness Viewed as a Gift and as a Quality," he writes,

---

[30] *Oxford University Sermons*, sermon 12, 236.
[31] Merrigan, "Revelation," 59.
[32] *Apologia*, 49.
[33] Bouyer, *Newman's Vision of Faith*, 168.

"Until Christ be Formed in You"

> Those who believe that Christ has set up a new creation in unity, and that He Himself is the One principle in His Church of all grace and truth, will not be surprised to find that He has superseded the righteousness, as He has abolished the victims, of the ancient time; and that as the grace of the Holy Eucharist is the Presence of Christ Crucified, so the justification of those who approach it is the Indwelling of Christ risen and glorified.[34]

One catches distinct resonances of Paul's awe-filled proclamation to the Colossians: "The mystery is this: Christ in you, the hope of Glory" (Col 1:27).

Jesus Christ justifies us by transforming us, by gracing us with a new relation to God, by incorporating us into his Body.

NEWMAN'S MYSTAGOGY: REALIZING CHRIST

For Newman, as we have seen, the Incarnation is the dogmatic principle *par excellence*, the Truth of God's Word become flesh in human history, the article of faith which distinguishes the Christian Church, upon which the Church stands or falls. In his *Lectures on Justification*, Newman vindicated this principle against an alternative which prevailed in many quarters of Protestantism. There, "justification by faith alone" appeared to be the decisive principle, the criterion of authentic Gospel preaching.

Newman held that this latter view smacked of subjectivism. Its outcome was to place emphasis upon the believer rather than upon the Object of belief, thereby usurping the place of Christ. In his final lecture "On Preaching the Gospel," he expresses his unease and his conviction in words that are as germane today as they were then:

> The fault here spoken of is the giving to our "experiences" a more prominent place in our thoughts than to the nature, attributes, and work of Him from whom they profess to come,— the insisting on them as a special point for the consideration of all who desire to be recognized as converted and elect. When men are to be exhorted to newness of life, the true Object to be put before them, as I conceive, is "Jesus Christ, the same yesterday, to-day, and for ever.[35]

---

[34] *Lectures on the Doctrine of Justification*, 201.
[35] Ibid., 325.

"Heart Speaks to Heart"

Note that Newman is certainly not arguing against exhorting men and women to "newness of life." Indeed, his sermons brim with such exhortation. His concern is when the criterion for such newness becomes one's own "experiences," one's passing "feelings," one's emotional highs, as we might say. In brief, he cautions against the pitfall of focusing upon one's salvation rather than upon the person of the Savior.

It may seem paradoxical that one who so stressed the importance of the heart and the affections should seemingly be suspicious of emotion. He himself allows that "no one (it is plain) can be religious without having his heart in his religion; his affections must be actively engaged in it; and it is the aim of all Christian instruction to promote this." But he dreads "lest a perverse use should be made of the affections." A singular display of this is the self-deception that "mere transient emotion" can substitute for true "obedience."[36] And so he concludes: "Let us take warning from Saint Peter's fall. Let us not promise much; let us not talk much of ourselves ... nor encourage ourselves in impetuous bold language in religion."[37]

A striking corollary of Newman's hermeneutic of suspicion regarding emotion bereft of reason is that the great preacher himself warns against putting excessive emphasis upon preaching—one that places undue burden upon the preacher to effect conversion, by devices that may even be manipulative, to the point of arousing frenzy. For Newman, the proper setting for preaching is within the objectivity of the Church's liturgy. Indeed, the cycle of the liturgical year and the readings designated for the celebrations provide the inspiration and frame for his sermons. Preaching is not an end in itself, but should ever orient towards worship, praise, and thanksgiving—in brief, towards God and not self. For, to stress again, "the true preaching of the Gospel is to preach Christ."[38]

To preach Christ, of course, is not merely to evoke a figure of the past, however much the earthly life, action, and teaching of Jesus is the indispensable point of reference for faith. It is to foster a real encounter with the living Lord, crucified, risen, and ascended who is truly present in his Church and its sacraments. In an Ascension

---

[36] Quotations are from the sermon, "Religious Emotion," in John Henry Newman, *Parochial and Plain Sermons* (London: Longmans, Green & Co., 1907), I, sermon 14, 179 (hereafter *PPS*).

[37] Ibid., 188.

[38] *Lectures on Justification*, 325.

sermon "Waiting for Christ," Newman insists that "[Christ] is the only Ruler and Priest in His Church, dispensing gifts, and has appointed none to supersede Him ... Christ's priests have no priesthood but His." In line with the Fathers of the Church, he is uncompromising: "when they baptize, He is baptizing; when they bless, He is blessing."[39]

Further, it would be a grievous error to understand Christ's Ascension as though he were no longer present to the Church and the believer. It is true that he is not present physically, as he was in first-century Galilee and Judea. But he is present spiritually, which for Newman signifies not less, but more truly present. In an Easter sermon "The Spiritual Presence of Christ in the Church," he insists

> [The Holy Spirit] has not so come that Christ does not come, but rather He comes that Christ may come in His coming ... The Holy Spirit causes, faith welcomes, the indwelling of Christ in the heart. Thus the Spirit does not take the place of Christ in the soul, but secures that place to Christ.[40]

Newman's own sermons, therefore, are "mystagogic" in that they not only preach Christ, they seek to introduce his hearers into some dimension of the mystery of Christ, to aid their entry into his mystery, to make it their own. He endeavors to midwife their "realization" of the mystery so that they might truly "put on Christ."

Newman uses that last phrase in another Easter sermon, "Difficulty of Realizing Sacred Privileges." In it, he shows his keen appreciation of the fact that we require time to come to know the import of our confession of faith, to mature in Christian living. And this is not only because of the impediments of human sinfulness, but because Christian faith so transcends our human earth-bound apprehension. God has raised Christ and has made us heirs of the Kingdom in Christ. Hence the need for steadfast perseverance in prayer, meditation, and work; hence the need for fidelity and obedience in daily exercises and practices. These seeming pedestrian virtues, and not fleeting sentiments or high-sounding words, are the gauge of spiritual seriousness. Thus, "waiting on God day by day, we shall make progress day by day, and approach to the true and clear view of what He has made us to be in Christ."[41]

---

[39] *PPS*, VI, sermon 17, 242.
[40] *PPS*, VI, sermon 10, 126.
[41] *PPS*, VI, sermon 8, 99.

"Heart Speaks to Heart"

Ian Ker makes an astute observation regarding the importance of "obedience" in Newman's spirituality and preaching. Ker writes, "not because obedience is more important than faith and love, but because it is the concrete proof and realization of things more important than itself, things only too easily corrupted or counterfeited."[42] In his piercing Advent homily "Unreal Words," Newman broaches forcefully one of his predominant spiritual concerns: namely, employing words and verbal professions that do not reflect the truth of one's lived engagements. He deplores "profession without action," and "speaking without seeing or feeling."[43] And this, for Newman, is to be "unreal"—the all too common condition of a fallen humanity and of a wayward world.

Jesus Christ, who is the very Truth of God Incarnate, first embodied and then spoke an integral Word. He brought to the world a "new language," not merely of words, but of actions, dispositions, and virtues. So Newman, in a splendid peroration, exhorts his hearers:

> It is not an easy thing to learn that new language which Christ has brought us. He has interpreted all things for us in a new way; He has brought us a religion which sheds a new light on all that happens. Try to learn this language. Do not get it by rote, or speak it as a thing of course. Try to understand what you say. Time is short, eternity is long; God is great, man is weak; [man] stands between heaven and hell; Christ is his Saviour; Christ has suffered for him.[44]

"New language, new way, new light!"—Newman clearly is imbued with the New Testament's awe-filled sense of the new beginning that Jesus Christ has brought and is: the new Adam.

Corresponding to this realization of eschatological newness is the persuasion in the New Testament and the Fathers of the radical transformation to which believers are called: not just a better self, a new self. Schooled in Scripture and the Fathers, Newman repeatedly refers to the "new creation" which Jesus Christ has inaugurated. Initiated in the new birth of Baptism, the Christian is destined to grow into the fullness of Christ, towards that "per-

---

[42] Ian Ker, "Introduction" in *John Henry Newman, Selected Sermons* (The Classics of Western Spirituality), ed. Ian Ker (New York: Paulist Press, 1994), 49.
[43] *PPS*, V, sermon 3, 42.
[44] Ibid., 44–5.

"Until Christ be Formed in You"

fection" which Paul in chapter three of Philippians holds to be the common goal to which disciples are bent.

In sermon after sermon, Newman takes pains to impress upon his hearers that the journey of faith is no joyride. Or rather that the surpassing joy is the end, not the starting point. How can it be other if, in the words of one of his most celebrated homilies, "The Cross of Christ" is, for Christian faith, "the Measure of the World?" In our present time, more than in Newman's day, even Christian theology frequently marginalizes the Cross, often viewing it as the unhappy consequence of a life disruptive of the "establishment."[45] Newman's words, then, are even more challenging and imperative. He insists "in the Cross, and Him who hung upon it, all things meet, all things subserve it, all things need it. It is their centre and their interpretation. For He was lifted upon it that He might draw all men and all things unto Him."[46] And he urges his hearers, "Let us begin with faith; let us begin with Christ; let us begin with His Cross and the humiliation to which it leads."[47]

In concluding this homily, Newman draws the inevitable implications of this doctrine, urging, as always, that believers realize the import of their profession, so that their words not remain "unreal":

> They alone are able to enjoy this world, who begin with the world unseen. They alone enjoy it, who have first abstained from it. They alone can truly feast, who have first fasted; they alone are able to use the world, who have learned not to abuse it; they alone inherit it, who take it as a shadow of the world to come, and who for that world to come relinquish it.[48]

Both in his day and in ours, there are some who object that Newman's vision in these sermons is too severe, too austere. In a Lenten sermon "The Yoke of Christ," he anticipates the objection. He speaks of those who would soften the scandal and gild the Cross. They attempt to attract to religion "by making it appear not difficult and severe." But he dismisses this strategy as "a deceit," just as Jesus himself rebuked Peter for his attempt to repudiate the Cross. Indeed, for the one who faithfully follows Jesus on his Way, the

---

[45] See the magisterial study of Fleming Rutledge, *The Crucifixion: Understanding the Death of Jesus Christ* (Grand Rapids, MI: Eerdmans, 2015).
[46] *PPS*, VI, sermon 7, 86.
[47] Ibid., 93.
[48] Ibid.

burden is "light": "But grace makes it so; in itself it is severe, and any form of doctrine which teaches otherwise forgets that Christ calls us to His yoke, and that yoke is a cross."[49]

Thus, time and again, Newman seeks to impress upon his congregation the cost of discipleship; and, though he readily acknowledges that no one, save God, can read another's heart, it is clear that he holds that many, even among baptized Christians, ignore the demands of the Gospel and are but lukewarm in their faith. How much more, then, does the "world" hold Christianity at a distance, perceiving it to be a threat to its own earth-bound stratagems and devices. The preacher contends that "the world, which chooses the broad way, in consequence hates and spurns the narrow way; and in turn our Blessed Lord, who has chosen for us the narrow way, hates, scorns, spurns, denounces the broad way."[50] These are words apt to cause serious discomfort for all advocates of (to use Bonhoeffer's indictment) "cheap grace" or, closer to home, a new, supposedly more merciful, "pastoral paradigm."

Newman is unyielding in stressing the newness of the Christian reality and the depth and scope of personal transformation it entails. Taking on Christ's yoke, taking on the mind of Christ, he says, "is the result of a change from a state of nature, a change so great as to be called a death or even a crucifixion of our natural state."[51] It is no less than a new creation. Small wonder, then, that, to use the provocative title of another of his sermons, religion is but "a weariness to the natural man."[52]

To characterize the new state and situation of the Christian that is the fruit of Christ's death and resurrection, Newman often recurs to a passage from Paul's Epistle to the Colossians. He cites it as the governing text for one of his sermons for the Feast of the Ascension: "Rising with Christ." I transcribe the passage in the translation that Newman himself uses. "If ye then be risen with Christ, seek those things which are above, where Christ sitteth on the right hand of God. Set your affection on things above, not on things on the earth. For ye are dead, and your life is hid with Christ in God" (Col 3:1–3).

---

[49] *PPS*, VII, sermon 8, 106–7.
[50] Ibid., 115.
[51] Ibid., 113.
[52] *PPS*, VII, sermon 2, 13–26.

"Until Christ be Formed in You"

Adept mystagogue that he is, Newman often proceeds by way of contrast. Thus, he first sketches the manner of existence of those whose hearts fail to follow Christ in their affections and commitments. In a graphic image, he depicts them as the crowd "thronging and hurrying along the broad way." And he elucidates, "They walk without aim or object ... [and] follow whatever strikes them and pleases them; they indulge their natural tastes."[53]

In clear counter position to the "crowd," the disciples of the ascended Lord, "exalted and transfigured with Him," strive "to live in heaven in their thoughts, motives, aims, desires, likings, prayers, praises, intercessions, even while they are in the flesh."[54] Newman recognizes, of course, that such "transfiguration" is never fully realized *in statu viatoris*, thus the importance for the wayfaring Christian of the virtues of patience and perseverance. So, to the tepid or half-hearted, he issues this urgent injunction:

> Start now with this holy season, and rise with Christ. See he offers you His hand; He is rising; rise with Him. Mount up from the grave of the old Adam; from grovelling cares, and jealousies, and fretfulness, and worldly aims; from the thraldom of habit. From the tumult of passion, from the fascinations of the flesh, from a cold, worldly, calculating spirit, from frivolity, from selfishness ... I am not calling on you to go out of the world, or to abandon your duties in the world, but to redeem the time ... in good measure to realize honestly the words of the text, to "set your affections on things above;" and to prove that you are His, in that your heart is risen with Him, and your life hid in Him.[55]

"You are His!" Newman's preaching and teaching far transcend any mere moralism. The obedience to which he exhorts his hearers is, in the root sense of the word, an earnest and attentive "listening to" their and his Lord in whom they will find blessedness and true joy. Yet, in another sermon, he cautions them: "It is not His loss that we love Him not, it is our loss. He is All-blessed, whatever becomes of us. He is not less blessed because we are far from Him. It is we who are not blessed, except as we approach Him, except as we are like Him, except as we love Him."[56]

---

[53] *PPS*, VI, sermon 15, 209.
[54] Ibid., 214.
[55] Ibid., 219–20. The phrase in the quotation, "to realize honestly," is Newman's insistent antidote to "unreal words and professions."
[56] *PPS*, VII, sermon 2, 25.

"Heart Speaks to Heart"

The obedience of faith is not to a precept, but to a Person, the Person of the Son of God. And its goal is not mere imitation, but participation in his own life. In effect, in his theology and spirituality, Newman recovered the ancient Christian tradition of *theosis* or divinization. In a fine essay on the influence of the Fathers of the Church on Newman, Brian Daley writes,

> Newman's emphasis on Jesus' divine identity, even in the midst of his human words and activities, leads him to make his own the distinctive Greek Patristic idea of salvation not simply as a change in the believer's relationship with God, thanks to the work of Jesus—as most Protestants had taught since Luther—but as actual transformation, as participation through the Spirit in the divine life and Trinitarian relationships of the Son.[57]

The thrust of the present essay has been not only to underscore Daley's remark, but to suggest further that, for Newman, deification is *Christification*. Just as justification is the indwelling of the risen Christ, so sanctification is progressively to be configured to and transfigured in Jesus Christ. I know of no bolder statement of this on Newman's part than his sermon, "Righteousness Not of Us, but in Us." There, he boldly asserts, in a passage I cannot forbear from quoting at length:

> What was actually done by Christ in the flesh eighteen hundred years ago, is in type and resemblance really wrought in us one by one even to the end of time. He was born of the Spirit, and we too are born of the Spirit. He was justified by the Spirit, and so are we. He was pronounced the well-beloved Son, when the Holy Ghost descended on Him; and we too cry Abba, Father, through the Spirit sent into our hearts. He was led into the wilderness by the Spirit; He did great works by the Spirit; He offered Himself to death by the Eternal Spirit; He was raised from the dead by the Spirit; He was declared to be the Son of God by the Spirit of holiness on His resurrection: we too are led by the same Spirit into and through this world's temptations; we, too, do our works of obedience by the Spirit; we die from sin, we rise again unto righteousness through the Spirit; and we are declared to be God's sons,—declared, pronounced, dealt with as righteous,—through our resurrection unto holiness in the Spirit. Or, to express the same great truth in other words;

---

[57] Brian E. Daley, "The Church Fathers," in *The Cambridge Companion to John Henry Newman*, 29–46, at 40.

"Until Christ be Formed in You"

> *Christ Himself vouchsafes to repeat in each of us in figure and mystery all that He did and suffered in the flesh. He is formed in us, born in us, suffers in us, rises again in us, lives in us.*[58]

CHRIST'S REAL PRESENCE

Some years ago, the literary and cultural critic George Steiner wrote a penetrating book, *Real Presences*. He sets forth his provocative thesis at the very beginning of his study:

> This essay proposes that any coherent understanding of what language is and how language performs, that any coherent account of the capacity of human speech to communicate meaning and feeling is, in the final analysis, underwritten by the assumption of God's presence. I will put forward the argument that the experience of aesthetic meaning in particular, that of literature, of the arts, of musical form, infers the necessary possibility of this "real presence."[59]

I can only imagine Newman vigorously nodding his assent, though he would accent what Steiner only hints at: the real presence in the world of the Incarnate Word.

I have previously cited Newman's splendid sermon, "The Spiritual Presence of Christ in the Church." Here, he expresses the very touchstone of his faith:

> Christ has promised He will be with us to the end—be with us, not only as He is in the unity of the Father and the Son, not in the Omnipresence of the Divine Nature, but personally, as the Christ, as God and man; not present with us locally and sensibly, but still really, in our hearts and to our faith. And it is by the Holy Ghost that this gracious communion is effected.[60]

The presence of the risen and ascended Christ is the very heart of the Church, founding, guiding, nourishing, and sustaining it in the midst of its journey to the fulfillment of God's promise.

Of course, the primordial sacrament of Christ's real presence is the Holy Eucharist. In his sermon "The Eucharistic Presence,"

---

[58] *PPS*, V, sermon 10, 139 (emphasis mine).
[59] George Steiner, *Real Presences* (Chicago: University of Chicago Press, 1989), 3.
[60] *PPS*, VI, sermon 10, 133.

"Heart Speaks to Heart"

Newman meditates upon Jesus' discourse on the Bread of Life in chapter 6 of St. John's Gospel. He expounds upon it in this fashion:

> The text speaks of the greatest and highest of all the Sacramental mysteries, which faith has been vouchsafed, that of Holy Communion. Christ, who died and rose again for us, is in it spiritually present, in the fullness of His death and of His resurrection. We call His presence in this Holy Sacrament a spiritual presence, not as if "spiritual" were but a name or mode of speech, and He were really absent, but by way of expressing that He who is present there can neither be seen nor heard; that He cannot be approached or ascertained by any of the senses; that He is not present in place, that He is not present carnally, though He is really present. And how this is, of course, is a mystery. All that we know or need know is that He *is* given to us, and that in the Sacrament of Holy Communion.[61]

It would be well to make two observations apropos of this affirmation of faith. First, Newman, as an Anglican, most certainly confessed Christ's real presence in the Eucharistic celebration and in the Holy Communion received by the faithful. Second, in his Anglican days, he was chary of the Roman Catholic doctrine of "transubstantiation," which he later professed as Catholic and admitted that he had not previously understood its true import.[62] However, it was only as a Catholic that he came to appreciate and draw immense spiritual sustenance from the real Presence of Christ in the reserved sacrament in Catholic churches throughout the world.[63]

In another sermon, "The Resurrection of the Body," Newman elucidates for his congregation the fruits of the Eucharist. "We eat the sacred bread, and our bodies become sacred; they are not ours; they are Christ's; they are instinct with that flesh which saw not corruption; they are inhabited by His Spirit; they become immortal; they die but to appearance, and for a time; they spring up when their sleep is ended, and reign with Him for ever."[64] And in an Easter sermon, "Christ, a Quickening Spirit," he speaks of "the

---

[61] *PPS*, VI, sermon 11, 136–7.
[62] See the careful discussion in Placid Murray, ed., *Newman the Oratorian* (Dublin: Gill & Macmillan, 1969), chapter three: "The Eucharistic Ministry."
[63] See John Tracy Ellis, "The Eucharist in the Life of Cardinal Newman," *Communio*, 4, no. 4 (Winter 1977), 320–40.
[64] *PPS*, I, sermon 21, 275.

blessed Sacrament of the Eucharist, in which Christ is 'evidently set forth crucified among us;' that we, feasting upon the Sacrifice, may be 'partakers of the Divine Nature.'"[65] Thus, the Eucharist effects in us what I earlier called *Christification*.

If, in his own day, Newman's theological-pastoral concern issued an urgent challenge to those who "discern not the Lord's Body,"[66] even among the many who attended Church; how much more would his concern be aroused today by the dramatic decline in Church attendance and, apparently, conviction concerning Christ's real presence in the Eucharist. We confront a dire situation which, sadly, lends credence to the discernment found in the subtitle of Louis Bouyer's book on Newman: "a time of general apostasy." Moreover, if Newman indicted his own culture's growing relativism, what would be his reaction to our contemporary culture that demonstrates so many tragic signs of being bereft of a sense of real presence and of wandering aimlessly in a wasteland of sheer absence: absence of meaning and of hope?

George Steiner, in *Real Presences*, speaks of our time as one of the "Epi-logue," the "After-word." The Logos, in which all things cohere and derive meaning, has faded in modern consciousness, and men and women are adrift in a disenchanted world. In his monumental study of modernity *A Secular Age*, the Catholic philosopher Charles Taylor, while appreciative of many of modernity's gains, forthrightly catalogues its weaknesses, indeed its despairing traits. He analyzes, for example, secularity's "immanent frame" in which all traces of a transcendent realm disappear in the wake of a frenetic consumerism. He also exposes modernity's "buffered self," insulated and isolated from relationships and commitments that might threaten individual autonomy. Finally, he diagnoses the malady of "excarnation," a profound dis-ease with the body, its fragility and ultimate mortality. And he urgently challenges his fellow Christians: "We have to struggle to recover a sense of what the Incarnation can mean."[67]

---

[65] *PPS*, II, 144..
[66] Ibid.
[67] Charles Taylor, *A Secular Age* (Cambridge, MA: Harvard University Press, 2007), 753. I confess to finding it odd that, in the book's more than eight hundred pages, there is no mention of John Henry Newman. For another insightful analysis of the spiritual plight of a disenchanted secular world, an age of "de-facement," see the English philosopher Roger Scruton's Gifford

"Heart Speaks to Heart"

John Henry Newman, then, appears a providential saint for our time, one who, in the midst of an incipient and spreading secularity, struggled successfully to recover and communicate creatively and imaginatively a profound sense of what the Incarnation means. And he does so, not least, by showing the profound links, in the Christian dispensation, between Incarnation and Eucharist. As he stated in one of his sermons, "no one realizes the Mystery of the Incarnation but must feel disposed towards that of Holy Communion."[68] For Christ's embodiment continues in his Eucharistic self-gift for the sake of his Body, the Church, and, through the Church, for the life of the world.

John Henry Newman is not only a saint, but a doctor for our contemporary plight, a guide out of the confinement of a one-dimensional world. He offers us an integral theological-spiritual vision whose Center is the Eucharistic Christ, the Christ whose being is to be Eucharist/Gift. Newman can serve as a God-inspired mentor, helping us to rekindle our Eucharistic imagination and to rejoice in Christ's real presence in the Eucharist, the paradigmatic expression of heart speaking to heart. He calls us to realize more fully Christ's gift of real presence and to join with him in joyful prayer, heart speaking to Heart:

> O most Sacred, most loving Heart of Jesus, you are concealed in the Holy Eucharist, and you beat for us still. Now, as then, you say: "With desire I have desired." I worship you with all my best love and awe, with my fervent affection, with my most subdued, most resolved will. O my God, when you condescend to suffer me to receive you, to eat and drink you, and for a while you take up your abode within me, make my heart beat with your Heart! Purify it of all that is earthly, all that is proud and sensual, all that is hard and cruel, of all perversity, of all disorder, of all deadness. So fill it with you, that neither the events of the day, nor the circumstances of the time, may have power to ruffle it, but that in your love and your fear, my heart may have peace. Amen.[69]

Lectures, *The Face of God* (London: Bloomsbury, 2012). He too, however, makes no mention of Newman.

[68] *PPS*, VI, sermon 11, 151.

[69] John Henry Newman, *Prayers, Verses, and Devotions* (San Francisco: Ignatius Press, 1989), 428. I have taken the liberty of changing Newman's original "thou's" to "you's." I should like to express my gratitude to the Reverend Richard G. Smith for his generous help in suggesting and locating sources.

9

Newman and Apologetics

Kevin J. O'Reilly

O N OCTOBER 11, 1845, just two days after St. John Henry Newman's reception into the Catholic Church, his sister Jemima wrote to her brother to express her profound concerns about his monumental decision to become a Roman Catholic, including the apparent "loss of influence" that, in her view, he would likely experience as a consequence of his conversion. Whereas he had previously "gained the ascendency" as an Anglican and "touched a chord" in all hearts "when you spoke in the name of our Church," she warned that her brother "will not influence the same class of minds that you have in times past. Believe me, it is very painful to me to contemplate all this, much more write it down."[1]

Three days later, John wrote back to his sister, responding that, whereas he was undeniably troubled by the pain that various individuals would likely undergo due to his decision, losing whatever prominence he had previously acquired was not a problem for him, as "the whole world is one great vanity, and I trust I am not set on any thing in it." Thereafter, in explaining further his resolution to convert, Newman conveyed to Jemima what, in many ways, were the central principles which guided not only his discernment in becoming a Catholic, but his entire life:

> With what conscience could I have remained? How could I have answered it at the last day, if, having opportunities of knowing

---

[1] Mrs. J. Mosely to Rev. J. H. Newman (October 11, 1845), in Anne Mozely, ed., *Letters and Correspondence of John Henry Newman during his Life in the English Church* (London: Longmans, Green & Co., 1903), II, 421.

the Truth which others have not, I had not availed myself of them? What a doom would have been mine, if I had kept the Truth a secret in my own bosom, and when I knew which the One Church was, and which was not part of the One Church, I had suffered friends and strangers to die in an ignorance from which I might have relieved them! Impossible. One may not act hastily and unsettle others when one has not a clear view—but when one has, it is impossible not to act upon it.[2]

In effect, how could he do otherwise? For Newman, he had no choice but to follow the truth upon ascertaining it and to share his discovery openly with others.

Here, in just a few sentences, Newman powerfully articulated what inspired his life's work and led him to the Catholic Church: his love of, quest for, and defense of truth. Since his youth, Newman had been devoted to truth and earnestly dedicated his whole life to it. For example, in August of 1824, Newman expressed in his private diary that "I think I really desire the truth, and would embrace it wherever I found it."[3] Years later, his classic intellectual autobiography *Apologia pro Vita Sua* was written in response to Charles Kingsley's biting comment in *MacMillan's Magazine* that "Truth, for its own sake, had never been a virtue with the Roman clergy. Father Newman informs us that it need not, and on the whole ought not to be."[4] In his famous 1879 *Biglietto* Speech delivered after being officially named a cardinal by Pope Leo XIII, Newman retrospectively described the central focus of his oeuvre as resistance to "liberalism in religion," which he defined as "the doctrine that there is no positive truth in religion, but that one creed is as good as another ... Revealed religion is not a truth, but a sentiment and a taste; not an objective fact, not miraculous; and it is the right of each individual to make it say just what strikes his fancy."[5] Indeed, his love of truth radiates from all of his sermons,

---

[2] John Henry Newman to Mrs. John Mosely (October 14, 1845), in Charles Steven Dessain *et al.*, eds., *The Letters and Diaries of John Henry Newman*, vols. I–XXXII (Oxford and London: Thomas Nelson, 1961–2008), XI, 16 (hereafter *LD*).

[3] John Henry Newman, "Autobiographical Memoir—Chapter 3," in Anne Mozely, ed., *Letters and Correspondence of John Henry Newman during his Life in the English Church*, I, 106.

[4] John Henry Newman to Messrs. Macmillan and Co. (December 30, 1863), in *LD*, XX, 571.

[5] John Henry Newman, "*Biglietto* Speech," in Rev. W.P. Neville, ed., *Addresses to*

writings and letters. As Joseph Ratzinger/Pope Benedict XVI notes, "truth is the central thought of Newman's intellectual grappling."[6]

Intimately connected with his fervor for truth (especially religious truth) was his dedication to defending the rational nature of Christianity. Diagnosing the adverse effects of secularization and many of the prevailing philosophical movements of his time, Newman deemed the status of religious faith in the nineteenth century as increasingly tenuous and set out in a variety of ways to establish the credibility of Christianity and, in particular, the Catholic faith. In fact, Ian Ker avers that Newman's primary intellectual concern was apologetic at its core:

> Newman certainly did not see himself as a theologian in any technical sense of the word. If he had an intellectual mission, apart from education, it lay in the field of apologetics—not in narrow polemic against Anglo-Catholics over the claims of Rome, but in a philosophical justification of "the Church and its position in the world in the nineteenth century as confronted with, and as against the penetrating knowledge, learning and ability of the scientific men and philosophers of the day."[7]

Thus, Newman's concern to justify the intelligibility of Christian belief was always "meant to show to those who had eyes to see that religious faith was not the expression of an irrational attitude or a purely arbitrary assumption."[8]

Apologetics is commonly understood as the rational defense of the truths of Christian faith through reason. The classical biblical expression of this idea is 1 Peter 3:15: "But in your hearts, reverence Christ as Lord. Always be prepared to make a defense to any one who calls you to account for the hope that is in you, yet do it with gentleness and reverence." The goal of apologetics is not to "prove" the tenets of Christianity apodictically as one does with a proposed solution to a mathematical problem, but to defend Christian teachings as credible, reasonable, and worthy of belief. In point of fact, Newman contends that apologetics can

---

Cardinal Newman with His Replies (London: Longmans, Green and Co., 1905), 64.

[6] Joseph Ratzinger, *On Conscience* (San Francisco: Ignatius Press, 2006), 24.

[7] Ian Ker, *John Henry Newman: A Biography* (Oxford: Oxford University Press, 2009), 463.

[8] Frederick Copleston, *A History of Philosophy*, vol. VIII, *Bentham to Russell* (New York: Doubleday, 1985), 510.

genuinely prepare the way for a person to make an act of faith by presenting a rationale that Catholicism is not only believable, but should be believed:

> Reason proves that Catholicism ought to be believed, and that in that form it comes before the Will, which accepts it or rejects it, as moved by grace or not. Reason does not prove that Catholicism is true, as it proves mathematical propositions are true; but it proves that there is a case for it so strong that we see we ought to accept it. There may be many difficulties, which we cannot answer, but still we see on the whole that the grounds are sufficient for conviction ... [W]hile there is enough evidence for conviction, whether we will be convinced or not, rests with ourselves.[9]

For Newman, apologetics can substantiate that Christian faith is credible. Whether an individual accepts Christianity as true or not is their own decision, but it can be demonstrated that belief is not an illogical or arbitrary judgment, but a reasonable conclusion. In addition, apologetics can also contribute to the decision for faith by clearing away potential obstacles or counterarguments that could hamper the effectiveness of the intellectual case for Catholicism: "surely, enough has been written—all the writing in the world would not destroy the necessity of faith ... The simple question is whether enough has been done to reduce the difficulties so far as to hinder them absolutely blocking the way, or excluding those direct and large arguments on which the reasonableness of faith is built."[10] Thus, apologetics can yield multiple benefits to those who evangelize and defend the Catholic faith and assist seekers of truth to find the ultimate object of their search in the person of Jesus Christ.

Nevertheless, Newman also grasped that any comprehensive apologetics must go beyond purely intellectual argumentation, because the means by which an individual subject recognizes truth involves several factors beyond what is strictly notional. In other words, Newman acknowledged that "after all, man is not a reasoning animal; he is a seeing, feeling, contemplating, acting animal"[11] and that there are numerous complex influences in play

---

[9] John Henry Newman to Catherine Ward (October 12, 1848), in *LD*, XII, 289.
[10] John Henry Newman to James Hope (November 20, 1850), in *LD*, XIV, 134.
[11] John Henry Newman, *Tamworth Reading Room*, in *Discussions and Arguments on Various Subjects* (London: Longmans, Green & Co., 1907), VI, 294.

when one determines that something or someone is credible. The intellect does not function in radical isolation and is impacted by suprarational dynamics such as personal attitudes, prior experiences, emotions, presuppositions, and moral outlooks. Actually, it is because of the effect of these antecedent determinants upon thought that one person can find a particular contention highly convincing, while another may consider the same point uncompelling.

In light of this, Newman held that apologetics, in order to defend the credibility of the Catholic faith persuasively, must not only present rational arguments, but also simultaneously appeal to the various dimensions of the believing subject which influence the recognition of truth. Indeed, Newman's own apologetics address not just the mind, but also the heart, which is not persuaded by solely intellectual means:

> The heart is commonly reached, not through the reason, but through the imagination, by means of direct impressions, by the testimony of facts and events, by history, by description. Persons influence us, voices melt us, looks subdue us, deeds inflame us. Many a man will live and die upon a dogma: no man will be a martyr for a conclusion.[12]

Ultimately, an act of faith is not the conclusion of a strictly rational process, but is due first and foremost to a gift of God's grace[13] which engages and invites a response of the whole person, including one's mind, heart, soul, freedom, conscience, emotions, imagination, and spirit. Therefore, from Newman's perspective, a purely rationalistic presentation of Christian truth will not be convincing on its own, as the intellect does not function in isolation from the affective dynamics which influence one's thought process. Any effective approach to defending the credibility of the Catholic faith must account for the complex ways in which a person comes to faith and thus address the multifaceted elements by which an individual subject deems something or someone to be believable.

In an 1870 letter to his friend Sister Mary Gabriel du Boulay, Newman offered three principle reasons or motivations behind

---

[12] *Ibid.*, VI, 293.
[13] In an 1870 letter, Newman replied to a correspondent that "if there is any definite question that I can answer you, I will do so—but I can't give the gift of faith." John Henry Newman to Mrs. Wilson (January 8, 1870), in *LD*, XXV, 6.

his writings: first, conversion; second, to "edify" Catholics (i.e., to improve their knowledge of their faith, since "many do not know their religion—many do not know the reason for it"); and, third, what he called "levelling up," or the raising all to "a better sort of religious sentiment ... the same moral and intellectual state of mind."[14] These three aims, which all revolve around conversion and deepening others' faith, are evident throughout all his works because Newman, having discerned the truth, always felt compelled to share and defend what he had ascertained in order to bring others to the Catholic faith or to buttress the faith of those who already believe.

To accomplish these goals, Newman found apologetics to be a valuable tool and, today, we can learn much from and emulate his impressive defense of the credibility of Catholicism. By all accounts, his apologetic program proved to be highly effective during his lifetime as Newman inspired many to follow him into the Catholic Church and, at present, many converts continue to cite him as a direct influence upon their decision to become Catholic. The questions which Christianity faces may change over time, but Newman's thought provides a reliable apologetic and guide as to how they can be answered convincingly.

The purpose of this paper is to present an overview of Newman's system of apologetics: how it is founded upon his religious epistemology and the multilevel process by which one makes an act of faith, and how it is simultaneously imaginative, personalist, and intellectual. It is hoped that this albeit brief exposition of Newman's multifaceted apologetics will demonstrate how Newman is, as Avery Dulles states in his magisterial work *A History of Apologetics*, the "leading Catholic apologist of the nineteenth century and one of the greatest of all time"[15] and in what manner his system of defending the Catholic faith can contribute to contemporary apologetics in our present twenty-first-century post-Christian culture.

---

[14] John Henry Newman to Sister Mary Gabriel du Boulay (January 2, 1870), in LD, XXV, 3.

[15] Avery Dulles, *A History of Apologetics* (San Francisco: Ignatius Press, 2005), 245.

Newman and Apologetics

ANTECEDENT PROBABILITIES AND THE ILLATIVE SENSE

As early as the 1820s, Newman recognized that the process by which a person identifies truth or even evaluates the credibility of a truth claim is not a strictly rational exercise. In fact, this realization hit close to home in that it largely emerged through his own personal interactions with members of his family. For example, in his diary entry of August 9, 1823, Newman describes a long argument which he had that day about religion with his increasingly skeptical younger brother Charles.[16] Despite John's best efforts to combat his brother's doubts, Charles announced in a letter to his brother some 18 months later that "I have come to a satisfactory conclusion with regard to religion ... I (after a great deal of preparatory thought, I acknowledge) have come to a judgment which no doubt will surprise you; for it is entirely against Christianity; which I expected to find synonymous with wisdom and knowledge, but which is far otherwise."[17]

In response, Newman wrote many extensive letters in an attempt to persuade Charles as to the truth of Christian faith. Yet, he quickly acknowledged that purely intellectual argumentation would not suffice, because his brother's repudiation of Christianity was rooted in pre-existing non-rational and emotional factors prior to the exercise of his intellect. The future saint's initial reply to Charles's letter noted quite frankly that "you are not in a state of mind to listen to argument of any kind"[18] and, three weeks later, he further explicated how it was his brother's underlying personal attitudes and not his intellect that had led him to repudiate Christian belief:

> I consider the rejection of Christianity to arise from a fault of the *heart*, not of the intellect; that unbelief arises, not from mere error of reasoning, but either from pride or from sensuality. It is important that at starting I should premise this, lest I should appear inconsistent, and to assert *both* that the Christian evidences are most convincing, *and yet* that they are not likely to convince those who reject them ... Hence the most powerful

[16] See Henry Tristram, ed., *John Henry Newman: Autobiographical Writings* (New York: Sheed and Ward, 1956), 192–3.
[17] Charles Newman to John Henry Newman (February 23, 1825), in *LD*, I, 212. For more information about Charles Newman's life, the influences on his thought and his relationship with his brother John, see Edward Short, *Newman and his Family* (London: T. & T. Clark, 2013), 115–39.
[18] John Henry Newman to Charles Newman (March 3, 1825), in *LD*, I, 212.

> arguments for Christianity do not *convince*, only *silence*; for there is at the bottom that secret antipathy for the doctrines of Christianity, which is quite out of the reach of argument. I do not then assert that the Christian evidences are *overpowering*, but that they are *unanswerable*; nor do I expect so much to show Christianity true, as to prove it *rational*; nor to prove infidelity *false*, so much as *irrational*.[19]

In Newman's view, no amount of evidence or rational arguments could ever be produced that would convince his brother of the veracity of Christianity without an anterior change in Charles's heart, attitude, and moral outlook.

In his *Fifteen Sermons Preached before the University of Oxford between A.D. 1826 and 1843*, Newman further explored these pre-rational dynamics and described them as "antecedent probabilities." Whereas the word probability may suggest a lack of certitude in certain contexts, Newman, inspired by his reading of Joseph Butler's 1736 work *The Analogy of Religion* and his maxim "probability is the guide of life,"[20] used the term to denote the various prior experiences, underlying assumptions, personal temperaments and moral attitudes that shape how we look at the world, filter and evaluate evidence, and make intellectual decisions. In an 1846 letter to his friend John Dalgairns, he clarified why he chose to describe these underlying factors with the nomenclature of probability:

> I use probable in opposition to "demonstrative"—and moral certainty is a *state of mind*, in all cases however produced by probable arguments which admit of more or less—the measure of probability necessary for certainty varying with the individual mind … [T]he great line of argument which *produces* moral certainty is not evidence, but antecedent probability.[21]

Matters of faith cannot be strictly proven or demonstrated logically, but rather require a moral certainty that is justified, for Newman, by probability. In addition, he deems these factors as "antecedent" in that they precede our individual acts of the intellect and

---

[19] John Henry Newman to Charles Newman (March 25, 1825), in *LD*, I, 219 (emphasis in original).

[20] See John Henry Newman, *Apologia pro Vita Sua* (London: Longmans, Green & Co., 1908), 7. Also, see Jane Garnett, "Joseph Butler," in Frederick D. Aquino and Benjamin J. King, eds., *The Oxford Handbook of John Henry Newman* (Oxford: Oxford University Press, 2018), 135–53.

[21] John Henry Newman to J. D. Dalgairns (December 8, 1846), in *LD*, XI, 289.

are "grounds which do not reach so far as to touch precisely the desired conclusion, though they tend towards it, and may come very near it."[22]

Throughout his *Oxford University Sermons*, he profoundly disagreed with the predominant "School of Evidences" approach to apologetics at Oxford at that time which emphasized strictly rational "proofs" of Christianity (as exemplified by William Paley and his famous "watchmaker" argument[23] and Richard Whately, an early colleague of Newman at Oriel College[24]). Newman, while not dismissing such intellectual arguments entirely, stressed their ineffectiveness when presented in isolation because they do not take into account the "antecedent considerations, presumptions, and analogies, which, vague and abstruse as they are, still are more truly the grounds on which religious men receive the Gospel."[25] In his view, these *a priori* antecedent probabilities are what a person utilizes in evaluating the cogency of the evidence for any *a posteriori* truth claim:

> Such alleged proofs are commonly strong or slight, not in themselves, but according to the circumstances under which the doctrine professes to come to us, which they are brought to prove; and they will have a great or small effect upon our minds, according as we admit those circumstances or not. Now, the admission of those circumstances involves a variety of antecedent views, presumptions, implications, associations, and the like, many of which it is very difficult to detect and analyze.[26]

Reasoned arguments for Christianity will be unpersuasive unless one prepares for their reception by taking into account these pre-rational factors which affect an individual's cognitive judgments. Indeed, in 1847, Newman composed a Latin preface to a proposed

---

[22] John Henry Newman, *Fifteen Sermons Preached Before the University of Oxford Between A.D. 1826 and 1843* (London: Longmans, Green & Co, 1909), sermon 12, 224 (hereafter *Oxford University Sermons*).

[23] See Dulles, *A History of Apologetics*, 187–90.

[24] See Geertjan Zuijdwegt, "Richard Whately," in Frederick D. Aquino and Benjamin J. King, eds., *The Oxford Handbook of John Henry Newman* (Oxford: Oxford University Press, 2018), 196–216. Years later, while studying in Rome, Newman encountered similar difficulties with the prevailing rationalistic Roman school of apologetics, led by Giovanni Perrone. See Dulles, *A History of Apologetics*, 242–4, 246.

[25] John Henry Newman, *Oxford University Sermons*, sermon 13, 264.

[26] Ibid., 273.

French translation of his *Oxford University Sermons* that succinctly sums up his position: *Praeambula fidei in individuis non cadunt sub scientiam* ("the preambles of faith in individuals do not fall under science").[27]

Drawing upon this theory of knowledge, Newman concludes that any decision either for or against Christian faith is ultimately an act of reason that is determined by one's antecedent probabilities. Although, both in Newman's day as in ours, it is often claimed that faith is opposed to reason, he cogently asserts in his sermon "Love the Safeguard of Faith against Superstition" that, in reality, non-believers utilize the same rational operation in rejecting God as believers do in accepting faith in God. Yet, both groups come to different conclusions due to these antecedent factors:

> As faith may be viewed as opposed to reason, in the popular sense of the latter word, it must not be overlooked that Unbelief is opposed to Reason also. Unbelief indeed, considers itself especially rational, or critical of evidence; but it criticizes the evidence of Religion, only because it does not like it, and really goes upon presumptions and prejudices as much as Faith does, only presumptions of the opposite nature.[28]

In this brilliant defense of the credibility of religious belief, an act of Christian faith is not irrational *in se*, but rather is the result of the same intellectual process involved in the denial of Christian faith. Unbelief is due to prior assumptions and preconceptions just as much as belief is. Both are acts of reason: the difference lies in one's antecedent probabilities.

To illustrate his point further, Newman analyzes David Hume's notorious argument against the historicity of miracles in the latter's *An Enquiry Concerning Human Understanding* and indicates that, in the end, Hume's renunciation of miracles is founded not upon a purely objective evaluation of the evidence, but rather his pre-existing view of the absolute impossibility of miracles. For Hume, this "antecedent improbability"[29] sufficed to refute all evidence in favor of the existence of miracles outright. Had he previously

---

[27] See Henry Tristam, ed., "Cardinal Newman's Theses *de Fide* and his Proposed Introduction to the French Translation of the University Sermons," *Gregorianum* 18 (1937), 252.

[28] John Henry Newman, *Oxford University Sermons*, sermon 12, 230.

[29] *Ibid.*, 231.

granted that miracles were actually possible, Hume certainly could have appraised the evidence as convincing and concluded differently. Consequently, religious faith, in Newman's view, cannot be deemed to be irrational while atheism is classified as rational, since both positions are the result of the same ratiocinative procedure. For Newman, faith is "an exercise of presumptive reasoning, or of Reason proceeding on antecedent grounds."[30]

However, he also identified a potential drawback with this position: that antecedent probabilities could be invoked to justify any viewpoint or system of "belief" (including superstition or even atheism) and result in the obscuring or even the rejection of objective truth. If one's individual subjective probabilities determine the adjudication of a truth claim, then two people could conceivably come to diametrically opposed conclusions and both be on seemingly solid epistemological ground, resulting in a chaotic relativism. Yet, Newman responds by asserting that, in point of fact, correct antecedent probabilities together with demonstrable evidence essentially enable the accurate recognition of objective truth:

> I would only maintain that that proof need not be the subject of analysis, or take a methodical form, or be complete and symmetrical, in the believing mind; and that probability is its life. I do but say that it is antecedent probability that gives meaning to those arguments from facts which are commonly called Evidences of Revelation; that, whereas mere probability proves nothing, mere facts persuade no one; that probability is to fact, as the soul to the body; that mere presumptions may have no force, but that mere facts have no warmth. A mutilated and defective evidence suffices for persuasion where the heart is alive; but dead evidence, however perfect, can but create dead faith.[31]

Neither probability without evidence nor evidence without probability is credible. Antecedent probabilities provide vitality and life to otherwise ineffectual evidence and, on the other hand, evidence and rational arguments prevent thought from slipping into extreme emotionalism and individualism.

---

[30] Ibid.
[31] Ibid., sermon 10, 199–200.

"Heart Speaks to Heart"

As beautifully expressed in the citation above, the key factor for Newman in the entire process of evaluating the truth claims of Christianity is a properly disposed heart, which makes possible both the recognition of credibility and the decision to believe:

> The safeguard of faith is a right state of heart. This is what gives it birth; it also disciplines it. This is what protects it from bigotry, credulity, and fanaticism. It is holiness, or dutifulness, or the new creation, or the spiritual mind, however we word it, which is the quickening and illuminating principle of true faith, giving it eyes, hands, and feet. It is Love which forms it out of the rude chaos into an image of Christ; or, in scholastic language, justifying faith, whether in Pagan, Jew, or Christian, is *fides formata charitate*.[32]

Love for God in one's heart opens the mind to recognize the truth and to make an act of faith. According to Newman, "faith is an act of reason, viz. a reasoning upon presumptions; right faith is a reasoning upon holy, devout, and enlightened presumptions … As far as, and wherever Love is wanting, so far, and there, faith runs into excess or is perverted."[33] Thus, it is a heart formed by love that recognizes objective truth and safeguards one from false belief. For this reason, Newman comments that the most common mistake made by unbelievers is "to think itself a judge of Religious Truth without preparation of the heart."[34] This insight became foundational to his entire approach to apologetics.

Newman's vision of how we identify truth was clearly contrary to the predominant Enlightenment rationalist view that intellectual objectivity demands the rejection of all prior assumptions and prejudices (e.g., René Descartes's methodology of systematic doubt). In a famous passage from his 1840 sermon "Implicit and Explicit Reason," Newman describes how antecedent probabilities, arguments and evidence all interact and enliven each other within the human mind as it evaluates what is true:

> The mind ranges to and fro, and spreads out, and advances forward with a quickness which has become a proverb, and a subtlety and versatility which baffle investigation. It passes on from point to point, gaining one by some indication; another on

---
[32] *Ibid.*, sermon 12, 234.
[33] *Ibid.*, 239.
[34] *Ibid.*, sermon 10, 198.

a probability; then availing itself of an association; then falling back on some received law; next seizing on testimony; then committing itself to some popular impression, or some inward instinct, or some obscure memory; and thus it makes progress not unlike a clamberer on a steep cliff, who, by quick eye, prompt hand, and firm foot, ascends how he knows not himself; by personal endowments and by practice, rather than by rule, leaving no track behind him, and unable to teach another. It is not too much to say that the stepping by which great geniuses scale the mountains of truth is as unsafe and precarious to men in general, as the ascent of a skillful mountaineer up a literal crag. It is a way which they alone can take; and its justification lies in their success. And such mainly is the way in which all men, gifted or not gifted, commonly reason,—not by rule, but by an inward faculty.[35]

Ian Ker, in commenting on this text, says that "no one surely has ever written more evocatively of the extraordinary power of the human mind."[36] Here, in opposition to the prevailing Enlightenment paradigm of the human mind as purely an impartial data processor, Newman beautifully illustrates how each person's intellect engages one's antecedent probabilities in assessing evidence within its multifaceted reasoning process. Clearly, Newman, in his understanding of how a person's preconceptions affect thought, considered that "antecedent probability is the great instrument of conviction in religious (nay in all) matters."[37]

Newman further explicates the role of antecedent probabilities in the adjudication of truth and certitude in his 1870 seminal work *An Essay in Aid of a Grammar of Assent* (hereafter *Grammar of Assent*). On December 3, 1877, Newman discussed the book with his fellow Oratorian Edward Caswall, who afterwards wrote his summary of Newman's stated assessment of his work on the flyleaf of his own copy: "Object of the book twofold. In the first part shows that you can believe what you cannot understand. In the second part that you can believe what you cannot absolutely prove."[38] Indeed,

---

[35] *Ibid.*, sermon 13, 257.
[36] Ker, *John Henry Newman: A Biography*, 263.
[37] John Henry Newman to W. G. Penny (December 13, 1846), in *LD*, XI, 293.
[38] See Charles Stephen Dessain, *John Henry Newman* (London: Thomas Nelson and Sons, 1966), 148. Also, see Charles Steven Dessain, "Cardinal Newman on the Theory and Practice of Knowledge: The Purpose of the *Grammar of Assent*," *Downside Review* 75 (1957), 1.

Newman seeks to justify Christian belief in his *Grammar of Assent* and indicates the trajectory that his work will follow by citing St. Ambrose's maxim *Non in dialecta complacuit Deo salvum facere populum suum* ("It did not please God to save his people through dialectic") on the front cover. Essential to Newman's argument in this text is his understanding of the illative sense, or the intellectual faculty of judgment that justifies belief in concrete propositions that cannot be logically demonstrated.

The term illative is derived from the Latin *illatus* (the perfect passive participle of the verb *infero*), signifying inference or the drawing of an inference. According to Newman, the illative sense is the intellectual capacity that determines a particular proposition as credible based upon the accumulation of various probabilities and multifaceted converging evidences. On this matter, Newman is greatly influenced by Aristotle and the understanding of *phronesis* in book six of his *Nicomachean Ethics*, which is the virtue of practical judgment in specific questions of morality and correct action:

> [Aristotle] calls the faculty which guides the mind in matters of conduct, by the name of *phronesis*, or judgment. This is the directing principle, controlling, and determining principle in such matters, personal and social. What it is to be virtuous, how we are to gain the just idea and standard of virtue, how we are to approximate in practice to our own standard, what is right or wrong in a particular case, for the answers in fullness and accuracy to these and similar questions, the philosopher refers us to no code of laws, to no moral treatise, because no science of life, applicable to the case of an individual, has been or can be written.[39]

In Aristotle's thought, *phronesis* is the practical moral virtue that guides the intellect in establishing right and wrong in various concrete situations. Similarly, Newman's illative sense denotes the faculty of practical judgment, but he expands its scope beyond the moral realm to encompass the search for truth in all areas.

In the *Grammar of Assent*, the most mature expression of his epistemology, Newman describes the illative sense as "right judgment in ratiocination,"[40] or the intellectual virtue which reviews

---

[39] John Henry Newman, *An Essay in Aid of a Grammar of Assent* (London: Longmans, Green & Co., 1903), 353–4.
[40] Ibid., 342.

one's antecedent probabilities together with discernable evidence and allows the intellect to draw certain conclusions about "what science cannot determine, the limit of converging probabilities and the reasons sufficient for a proof. It is the ratiocinative mind itself ... by which we are able to determine, and thereupon to be certain, that a moving body left to itself will never stop, and that no man can live without eating."[41] Because of one's illative sense, a person infers that converging probabilities warrant certitude and the intellect can thereby assent to concrete propositions as true. Newman cogently compares the strength of numerous congruent evidences and probabilities to that of "a cable which is made up of a number of separate threads, each feeble, yet together as sufficient as an iron rod."[42] In a famous instance of this dynamic from his *Grammar of Assent*, one can be legitimately certain that Great Britain is an island without actually circumnavigating it because of the numerous coinciding evidences and probabilities which substantiate the truth of the statement.[43]

Because of the illative sense, numerous similar conclusions are made by the mind regularly and are considered certain. In fact, Newman describes as "remarkable" how often, even in the sciences or "in cases where nothing stronger than presumption was ever professed, scientific men have sometimes acted as if they thought this kind of argument, taken by itself, decisive of a fact which was in debate."[44] Thus, the illative sense, which Newman deems "a grand word for a common thing,"[45] is central to his epistemology,[46]

---

[41] Ibid., 360.
[42] John Henry Newman to J. Walker of Scarborough (July 6, 1864), in *LD*, XXI, 146.
[43] See Newman, *Grammar of Assent*, 189–90, 294.
[44] Ibid., 383.
[45] John Henry Newman to Charles Meynell (November 17, 1869), in *LD*, XXIV, 375.
[46] For more extensive treatments of Newman's views on epistemology and religious faith, see Frederick Aquino, "Epistemology," 375–94; Frederick Copleston, "John Henry Newman," 510–25; Anthony Kenny, "Newman as a Philosopher of Religion," in David Brown, ed., *Newman: A Man for Our Time* (Harrisburg, PA: Morehouse Publishing, 1990), 98–122; Ian Ker, *The Achievement of John Henry Newman* (Notre Dame, IN: University of Notre Dame Press, 1990), 35–73; Basil Mitchell, "Newman as a Philosopher," in Ian Ker and Alan Hill, eds., *Newman after a Hundred Years* (Oxford: Clarendon Press, 1990), 223–46; Thomas Norris, "Faith," in Ian Ker and Terrence Merrigan, eds., *The Cambridge Companion to John Henry Newman* (Cambridge: Cambridge

his understanding of how a person comes to religious faith, and even how the human mind's capacity goes well beyond purely logical reasoning.[47]

NEWMAN'S FRAMEWORK FOR APOLOGETICS

How Newman's understanding of antecedent probabilities and the illative sense ground his apologetic defense of the Catholic faith is evident in a touching letter which he wrote to Louisa Simeon, the eldest daughter of his friend and fellow convert Sir John Simeon. After a devout upbringing and even a brief period of discernment of a possible vocation with the Benedictines, Louisa, at the age of twenty-six, had been undergoing troubling doubts about her Catholic beliefs because of her interactions with and questions from her mostly Protestant and non-believing friends. Newman gently responded to her struggles with faith by directing her toward the endeavor that guided his entire life: the search for truth. He suggested that she first investigate the difficult question of what is true regarding God and religion: "you must begin all thought about religion by mastering what is the fact, that any how the question has an inherent, irradicable difficulty in it." In answering this challenging question, she must assess "whether on

---

University Press, 2009), 73–97; Anselm Ramelow, "Knowledge and Normality: Bl. John Henry Newman's *Grammar of Assent* and Contemporary Skepticism," *Nova et Vetera* 11 (2013), 1081–1114.

[47] Many commentators hold that Newman anticipates the later views of Ludwig Wittgenstein, who read the *Grammar of Assent* and directly mentions Newman in the first paragraph in his *On Certainty*: "On this a curious remark ["eine komische Bemerkung"] by H. Newman." See Ludwig Wittgenstein, *On Certainty* (Oxford: Basil Blackwell, 1969), 2. For an overview of recent scholarly investigations into the connections between these two thinkers, see José Maria Ariso, "*Usum non tollit abusus*: La noción wittgensteiniana de 'certeza' a la luz de la *Gramatica del Asentimiento* del Cardenal Newman," *Estudios filosoficos* 61 (2012), 277–94; Angelo Bottone, "Newman and Wittgenstein after Foundationalism," *New Blackfriars* 86 (2005), 62–75; Wolfgang Kienzler, "Wittgenstein and John Henry Newman on Certainty," *Grazer philosophische studien* 71 (2006), 117–38; Duncan Pritchard, "Wittgenstein on Faith and Reason: The Influence on Newman," in Miroslaw Szatkowski, ed., *God, Truth, and Other Enigmas* (Berlin: De Gruyter, 2015), 197–216; Friedo Ricken, "Wittgenstein und Newman über die Krise des religiösen Glaubens in der westlichen Zivilisation," in Rainer Berndt, ed., *Vernünftig* (Würzburg: Echter, 2003), 67–80.

the whole our reason does not tell us that it is a duty to accept the arguments commonly urged for its truth as sufficient, and a duty in consequence to believe heartily in Scripture and the Church." Thus, the intellect can bring one to the point of recognizing the sufficiency of the substantiation for faith and the duty to assent to what is true: a duty which suggests "something or some one to which it is to be referred, to which we are responsible. That something that has dues upon us is God."[48]

However, Newman thereafter recommended to Louisa where the proper starting point for religious inquiry is:

> You must not suppose that I am denying the intellect its real place in the discovery of truth; but it must be ever borne in mind that its exercise mainly consists in reasoning,—that is, in comparing things, classifying them, and inferring. It ever needs points to start from, first principles, and these it does not provide—but it can no more move one step without these starting points, than a stick, which supports a man, can move without the man's action ... [W]e have to ascertain the starting points for arriving at religious truth ... To gain religious starting points, we must ... interrogate our hearts, and (since it is a personal, individual matter) our own hearts,—interrogate our own consciences, interrogate, I will say, the God who dwells there.[49]

Newman tenderly encouraged Luisa to begin her investigation into the truth of her faith with her heart and to find God's voice and presence in her conscience. At the end of the letter, he further appealed to other antecedent probabilities by counseling her to pray and meditate on the Scriptures "with an earnest desire to know the truth and a sincere intention in following it."[50]

Newman's strategy clearly was to prepare Louisa's antecedent probabilities so that she, utilizing her illative sense, would be able to evaluate the accumulated rational evidence for the Catholic faith and judge Catholicism to be true. Joyce Sugg, in commenting on this letter, writes that "this was wise counseling of a high order and Louisa Simeon seems to have discovered an adult faith as a result."[51]

---

[48] John Henry Newman to Louisa Simeon (June 25, 1869), in *LD*, XXIV, 275.
[49] Ibid., 275–6.
[50] John Henry Newman to Louisa Simeon (June 25, 1869), in *LD*, XXIV, 276.
[51] Joyce Sugg, *Ever Yours Affly: John Henry Newman and his Female Circle* (Leominster: Gracewing, 1996), 273.

"Heart Speaks to Heart"

Newman's perspective on how the mind discerns truth through antecedent probabilities and the illative sense undergirds the methodology which he deemed to be the most effective framework for explicating and defending Christianity and the Catholic faith: namely, appealing to the antecedent probabilities which directly affect and empower the assessment of credibility while simultaneously accumulating multiple converging evidences and arguments which testify to the truth of Catholicism. While attention to both pre-rational factors as well as evidential corroboration are needed, the antecedent probabilities are the key determinants in Newman's strategy for apologetics, as they vivify the coherence of the discernable data and intellectual arguments and make the adjudication of certitude possible. Newman had parted ways with the ascendant "Evidentialist School" of apologetics of his time not due to any type of dismissal of rational argumentation *in se*, but, as Avery Dulles asserts, "in insisting on the importance of the moral and religious dispositions with which we interpret the data."[52] The indispensable component in the recognition of the cogency of any truth claim is precisely one's properly disposed antecedent probabilities, without which no amount of evidence will appear credible. In the *Grammar of Assent*, Newman clearly states that purely intellectual arguments will not persuade without an appeal to the larger ratiocinative process in which the mind functions: "if I am asked to convert others by a smart syllogism, I say plainly I do not care to overcome their reason without touching their hearts."[53] For Catholic apologetics to be effective, one must inspire such antecedent probabilities as a correctly disposed heart and will, good intentions and appropriate moral outlook in order for the objective truth claims of Catholicism to become evident through one's illative sense.

Thus, for Newman, antecedent probabilities are the primary influences in the discernment of the truth and any persuasive apologetics for the Catholic faith must engage these multifaceted dimensions which serve as the starting points for the intellectual acceptance of the truth. As he stated in a letter to Edward Healy

---

[52] Avery Dulles, *Newman* (London: Continuum, 2002), 42.
[53] Newman, *Grammar of Assent*, 425.

Thompson in 1853, recognizing the importance of antecedent probabilities "is how you convert factory girls as well as philosophers."[54]

Newman's apologetics follow a multilevel interrelated schema that appeals to one's antecedent probabilities and is simultaneously imaginative, personalist, and intellectual. For Newman, the imaginative and personalist dimensions of his apologetics target the heart, while his brilliant rational arguments appeal to the intellect that has been rightly enlivened by one's antecedent probabilities. Despite space constraints here, all three dimensions are worthy of brief review.

First, concerning the imagination, Newman describes it as the faculty that makes one's faith real or gives life to purely notional ideas. In his *Grammar of Assent*, he outlines how a dogma of faith "is discerned, rested in, and appropriated as a reality, by the religious imagination"[55] and thereby becomes a vivid influence upon one's life and behavior. It is through the imagination that one can answer affirmatively to the questions "Can I attain to any more vivid assent to the Being of God, than that which is given merely to notions of the intellect? … Can I rise to what I have called an imaginative apprehension of it? Can I believe as if I saw?"[56] Even the theoretical acceptance of the statement "there is a God" will only effect "living mastery" in one's life and "a revolution in the mind" once it is "addressed to the imagination."[57] In fact, Newman deemed the role of imagination as so crucial in the decision to believe that he wrote in 1857 that "imagination, not reason, is the great enemy of faith"[58] if it is not appropriately oriented towards the truth.

Newman makes numerous apologetic appeals to the imagination throughout his works, but, according to Ian Ker, he dedicated four works in particular to "imaginative apologetics": his two novels *Loss and Gain* and *Callista*, and two collections of lectures (*Lectures on Certain Difficulties Felt by Anglicans in Submitting to the Catholic Church* and *Lectures on the Present Position of Catholics in*

---

[54] John Henry Newman to Edward Healy Thompson (June 12, 1853), in *LD*, XV, 381.
[55] Newman, *Grammar of Assent*, 98.
[56] Ibid., 102.
[57] Ibid., 126.
[58] Hugo Achaval and J. Derek Holmes, eds., *The Theological Papers of John Henry Newman on Faith and Certainty* (Oxford: Clarendon Press, 1976), 47.

England).⁵⁹ For example, in his 1848 novel *Loss and Gain*, his first work after his conversion to the Catholic Church, he tells the story of a Catholic convert, Charles Reding, and, at the conclusion of the novel, Newman beautifully expresses the peace that the protagonist experiences after his reception into the Catholic Church:

> It was Sunday morning about seven o'clock, and Charles had been admitted into the communion of the Catholic Church about an hour since. He was still kneeling in the church of the Passionists before the Tabernacle, in the possession of a deep peace and serenity of mind, which he had not thought possible on earth. It was more like the stillness which almost sensibly affects the ears when a bell that has long been tolling stops, or when a vessel, after much tossing at sea, finds itself in harbour. It was such as to throw him back in memory on his earliest years, as if he were really beginning life again. But there was more than the happiness of childhood in his heart; he seemed to feel a rock under his feet; it was the *soliditas Cathedrae Petri*. He went on kneeling, as if he were already in heaven, with the throne of God before him, and angels around, and as if to move were to lose his privilege.⁶⁰

Such sublime imagery appeals to the imagination and invites any seeker of truth, solace and inner tranquility to open his or her mind to consider the Catholic faith as the ultimate fulfillment of their search.

Secondly, Newman's apologetics and his entire thought are also keenly personalist. Edward Sillem, in assessing the influence of Newman's multifaceted personalism, proposes that "he stands at the threshold of the new age as a Christian Socrates, the pioneer of a new philosophy of the individual Person and Personal Life."⁶¹ In many ways, it can be said that Newman's cardinalatial motto *Cor ad cor loquitur* ("heart speaks to heart") expresses a deeply per-

---

59   See Ian Ker, "John Henry Newman: Analogy, Image, and Reality," *Newman Studies Journal* 12 (2015), 15–32. Other excellent studies on Newman's reflections on the role of imagination include Bernard Dive, *John Henry Newman and the Imagination* (London: T. & T. Clark, 2018), and Terrence Merrigan, "The Imagination in the Life and Thought of John Henry Newman," *Cahiers Victoriens et Édouardiens* 70 (2009), 187–217.

60   John Henry Newman, *Loss and Gain: The Story of a Convert* (London: Longmans, Green & Co., 1906), 430.

61   Edward Sillem, *The Philosophical Notebook* (Louvain: Nauwaelerts, 1961), I, 250.

sonalist vision of the human person, humanity's relationship with God, and how the faith is transmitted from one person to another. According to Louis Bouyer, Newman holds that "it is as a person that God reveals himself,"[62] especially as God speaks directly to each person's conscience. In opposition to various nineteenth-century Enlightenment and Romanticist intellectual movements that presented overly rationalistic and reductionist views of the humanity, Newman maintains the innate dignity of each human person as a concrete individual who is addressed personally by the Tri-personal God.

Furthermore, he stresses that a personalist approach is the most effective way in transmitting the faith from one individual to another. In his 1832 sermon "Personal Influence, the Means of Propagating the Truth," Newman outlines how personal testimony has historically overcome all obstacles down through the centuries and successfully handed on Christian faith and life to countless believers:

> Such, then, are the difficulties which beset the propagation of the Truth: its want of instruments, as an assailment of the world's opinions; the keenness and vigour of the weapons producible against it, when itself in turn is to be attacked. How, then, after all, has it maintained its ground among men, and subjected to its dominion unwilling minds, some even bound to the external profession of obedience, others at least in a sullen neutrality, and the inaction of despair? I answer, that it has been upheld in the world not as a system, not by books, not by argument, nor by temporal power, but by the personal influence of such men as have already been described, who are at once the teachers and the pattern of it.[63]

In addition, as John Crosby illustrates in his illuminating study of Newman's personalism, he always spoke tenderly from his heart in order to communicate with others' hearts, most especially in his homilies and letters. His motto "heart speaks to heart" reflects Newman's own comprehensive "way of being, or more exactly, to a personalist way of speaking. There is a mysterious affective tenderness in Newman's words, a power to pierce the heart of

---

[62] Louis Bouyer, *Newman: An Intellectual and Spiritual Biography* (San Francisco: Ignatius Press, 2011), 28.
[63] John Henry Newman, *Oxford University Sermons*, sermon 5, 91–2.

those whom he addresses, a power to sympathize with them."[64] This personalist dynamic to Newman's thought and interpersonal relations constitutes an effective facet of his overall apologetics and helped him to inspire many to accept the Catholic faith.

Lastly, Newman offers numerous intellectual defenses of Christianity throughout his entire corpus that powerfully testify to the truth of the Catholic faith. Once a person's antecedent probabilities are vivified properly through the imagination and personalist appeals to the heart, the aggregation of various evidences attesting to the rational nature of Christianity has the cumulative effect of tying smaller corroborating strands together into a mighty apologetic cord and, for Newman, contributes to the functioning of one's illative sense and the recognition of Catholicism as true.

Many of his Newman's works are now justifiably considered classics in the field of apologetics and are interwoven with manifold rational defenses for religious belief itself, Christianity, and the Catholic faith in particular. His *Oxford University Sermons* explicate his views on the relationship between Christian faith and reason and, as outlined earlier, defend the act of Christian faith as truly an exercise of reason. He defends the existence, historicity and biblical evidence for the historicity of miracles (especially against Hume's well-known arguments to the contrary) and delineates how to distinguish between authentic and supposed pagan miracles in two early essays which were later republished in 1870 as *Two Essays on Biblical and Ecclesiastical Miracles*. In *An Essay on the Development of Christian Doctrine*, Newman delineates his understanding of how Church teaching develops and proposes a series of seven tests or "notes" to ascertain when true doctrinal development has taken place as opposed to corruption. His detailed historical analysis of the Catholic Church's doctrinal teachings and their organic consistency converge upon the conclusion that only the Roman Catholic Church is the authentic successor of the early Church: "If then there is now a form of Christianity such, that it extends throughout the world ... that amid disorders and fears there is one Voice for whose decisions the peoples wait with trust, one Name

---

[64] John F. Crosby, *The Personalism of John Henry Newman* (Washington, DC: Catholic University of America Press, 2014), 87. Also, see David Whalen, *The Consolation of Rhetoric: John Henry Newman and the Realism of Personalist Thought* (San Francisco: Catholic Scholars Press, 1994).

and one See to which they look with hope, and that name Peter, and that see Rome;—such a religion is not unlike the Christianity of the fifth and sixth centuries."[65]

Newman's 1864 *Apologia pro Vita Sua*, his personal account of his theological journey to Catholicism, describes how, from his initial religious awakening at the age of fifteen, he had discerned the existence of "two and two only absolute and luminously self-evident beings, myself and my creator."[66] He developed this insight further with his acclaimed argument for God's existence from conscience, which "implies that there is One to whom we are responsible, before whom we are ashamed, whose claims on us we fear."[67] In fact, the accumulation of evidence which he uncovered in his investigation into the development of doctrine coalesced with his experience of God in his conscience and led to his decision to become Catholic:

> I was led on to examine more attentively ... the concatenation of argument by which the mind ascends from its first to its final religious idea; and I came to the conclusion that there was no medium, in true philosophy, between Atheism and Catholicity, and that a perfectly consistent mind, under those circumstances in which it finds itself here below, must embrace either the one or the other. And I hold this still: I am a Catholic by virtue of my believing in a God; and if I am asked why I believe in a God, I answer that it is because I believe in myself, for I feel it impossible to believe in my own existence (and of that fact I am quite sure) without believing also in the existence of Him, who lives as a Personal, All-seeing, All-judging Being in my conscience.[68]

Also, he argues that the widespread prevalence of sin counterintuitively serves as evidence for God's existence, because it indicates that humanity is "implicated in some terrible aboriginal calamity" and "out of joint with the purposes of its creator"; thus, "the doctrine of what is theologically called original sin becomes to me almost as certain as that the world exists, and as the existence of God."[69]

---

[65] John Henry Newman, *An Essay on the Development of Christian Doctrine* (London: Longman, Green & Co., 1909), 321–2.
[66] Newman, *Apologia pro Vita Sua*, 3.
[67] Newman, *Grammar of Assent*, 109.
[68] Newman, *Apologia pro Vita Sua*, 129.
[69] Ibid., 158.

In his *Grammar of Assent*, Newman develops further the connection of sin with religious belief itself and explicates how all religions, natural and revealed, are founded upon an existential "sense of sin and guilt, and without this sense there is for man, as he is, no genuine religion."[70] There is a universally prevalent sense that something is wrong with the world and religious faith expresses hope for deliverance. For Newman, natural religion itself serves as an antecedent probability for the recognition of the truth of divine revelation and, in fact, Christianity is "the completion and supplement of Natural Religion, and of previous revelations."[71] He stresses that "one of the most important effects of Natural Religion on the mind, in preparation for Revealed, is the anticipation which it creates, that a Revelation will be given. That earnest desire of it, which religious minds cherish, leads the way to the expectation of it."[72] Natural religion "recognizes the disease, but it cannot find, it does but look out for the remedy. That remedy, both for guilt and moral impotence, is found in the central doctrine of Revelation, the Mediation of Christ."[73]

Over the final hundred or so pages of the *Grammar of Assent*, Newman assembles an impressive series of historical evidences which, for the intellect guided by its illative sense, converge upon the conclusion that Catholicism is true. Methodologically, Newman prefers "to rely on that of an accumulation of various probabilities …, that from probabilities we may construct legitimate proof, sufficient for certitude."[74] He lists such evidences as fulfilled prophecies, miracles, Church history, Patristic texts, etc., as providing converging substantiation of the truth of the Catholic faith. During his presentation, Newman examines Edward Gibbon's proposed naturalistic reasons for the success of Christianity in *The Decline and Fall of the Roman Empire* and finds them inadequate to account for the propagation of the Catholic faith. Instead, Newman counters that the true conversion and zeal at the heart of Christian belief can only be explained through Christ, who

> imprinted the Image or idea of Himself in the minds of His subjects individually; and that Image, apprehended and worshipped in

---

[70] Newman, *Grammar of Assent*, 400.
[71] Ibid., 388.
[72] Ibid., 422–3.
[73] Ibid., 487.
[74] Ibid., 411.

> individual minds, becomes a principle of association, and a real bond of those subjects one with another, who are thus united to the body by being united to that Image; and moreover that Image, which is their moral life, when they have been already converted, is also the original instrument of their conversion. It is the Image of Him who fulfills the one great need of human nature, the Healer of its wounds, the Physician of the soul, this Image it is which both creates faith, and then rewards it.[75]

Ultimately, only divine grace and the love of and for Christ can fully account for the Catholic faith and its growth through the centuries.[76]

Whereas certain individual works may focus on one particular aspect of his apologetic vision, Newman's system of defending Christian belief, to be appreciated rightly and fully, must be taken as an integral whole while keeping in balance the respective roles of antecedent probabilities, the illative sense, evidences, and intellectual argumentation. Newman's apologetics address the whole person, and no one facet will be particularly effective in isolation from the others. For example, while outlining his cogent arguments for God's existence, he concedes that purely notional demonstrations will not inspire belief:

> I am far from denying the real force of the arguments in proof of a God, drawn from the general facts of human society and the course of history, but these do not warm me or enlighten me; they do not take away the winter of my desolation, or make the buds unfold and the leaves grow within me, and my moral being rejoice.[77]

Consequently, Newman's brilliant framework for apologetics, which certainly is worthy of further detailed studies, should always be understood holistically in terms of its interrelated imaginative, personalist and intellectual dynamics which are enlivened by antecedent probabilities.

---

[75] *Ibid.*, 464.
[76] For more detailed expositions of Newman's intellectual apologetics, see Avery Dulles, *A History of Apologetics*, 245–50; Ian Ker, *The Achievement of John Henry Newman*, 35–73, 96–151; Matthew Levering, *Proofs of God: Classical Arguments from Tertullian to Barth* (Grand Rapids, MI: Baker Publishing, 2016), 144–9; Jan Henrik Walgrave, *Newman the Theologian: The Nature of Belief and Doctrine as Exemplified in His Life and Works* (London: Geoffrey Chapman, 1960), 199–240.
[77] John Henry Newman, *Apologia pro Vita Sua*, 157.

"Heart Speaks to Heart"

CONCLUSION

On October 2, 1873, the future cardinal and Saint John Henry Newman delivered his prescient sermon "The Infidelity of the Future" at the dedication of St. Bernard's Seminary at Olton near Birmingham, during which he predicted an upcoming widespread "infidelity" unlike any that Christian faith had encountered before. Prophetically anticipating many of the difficult challenges facing the Catholic Church in the twenty-first century, Newman forecast that the intellectual Zeitgeist of this upcoming period will deny the very rationality of the foundations of religious belief itself:

> There is no revelation from above. There is no exercise of faith. Seeing and proving is the only ground of believing. They go on to say, that since proof admits of degrees, a demonstration can hardly be had except in mathematics; we never can have simple knowledge; truths are only probably such. So that faith is a mistake in two ways. First, because it usurps the place of reason, and secondly because it implies an absolute assent to doctrines, and is dogmatic, which absolute assent is irrational. Accordingly, you will find, certainly in the future, nay more, even now, even now, that the writers and thinkers of the day do not believe there is a God. They do not believe either the object—a God personal, a Providence and a moral Governor; and secondly, what they do believe, viz., that there is a first cause or other, they do not believe with faith, absolutely, but as a probability.[78]

As opposed to previous ages which, while at times hostile to Christian faith, still generally acknowledged the existence of such fundamental truths as a moral law, "Christianity has never yet had experience of a world simply irreligious … But we are now coming to a time when the world does not acknowledge our first principles."[79] According to Newman, the Church will face a "darkness different in kind from any that has been before it" and that would appall "even such courageous hearts as St. Athanasius, St. Gregory I, or St. Gregory VII."[80]

---

[78] John Henry Newman, "The Infidelity of the Future," in *Faith and Prejudice and Other Unpublished Sermons* (New York: Sheed and Ward, 1956), 124.
[79] Ibid., 124–5.
[80] Ibid., 117.

Newman and Apologetics

Remarkably, Newman not only foresaw in 1873 much of the twenty-first-century postmodern Weltanschauung and its denial of objective truth, but also adumbrated how faithful Christians should respond: with an emphasis on truth. First, he encouraged believers to "gain the habit that we are in God's presence," as the realization of the truth of God's immanence will prevent undue attachments and "thus an elevation of mind will be created ... against the infidelity of the world."[81] Secondly, Newman encouraged all to gain "sound, accurate, complete knowledge of Catholic theology":

> Because the world is full of doubtings and uncertainty, and of inconsistent doctrine—a clear consistent idea of revealed truth, on the contrary, cannot be found outside of the Catholic Church. Consistency, completeness, is a persuasive argument for a system being true. Certainly if it be inconsistent, it is not truth.[82]

Not surprisingly, truth, which was always at the heart of Newman's life and work, provides the core of his recommendations for Catholics living in a radically secularized world and, as during his own lifetime, Newman's apologetics can serve the cause of truth today by indicating that the Catholic faith is credible, worthy of belief, and true.

In recent decades, there has been a revival of apologetics in both Catholic and Protestant circles, with different apologetic schools championing varying methodologies.[83] Among the current models, Newman's apologetic system most resembles the "Cumulative Case" school, which emphasizes that the totality of the multifaceted evidence for Christian belief provides the most credible and rational explanation of reality. Nevertheless, given the predominance of postmodernism in our current intellectual and cultural landscape, many Catholic thinkers, including Avery Dulles, have observed that "the time is ripe, the need is urgent, for a rebirth of apologetics."[84] Because of the large-scale renunciation

---

[81] *Ibid.*, 127.
[82] *Ibid.*, 128.
[83] For an overview of the development of contemporary apologetics and its varying approaches, see Avery Dulles, *A History of Apologetics*, 271–367; Stanley Gundry and Steven Cowan, *Five Views on Apologetics* (Grand Rapids, MI: Zondervan, 2000); Gordon Lewis, *Testing Christianity's Truth Claim* (Chicago: Moody Press, 1976); Bernard Ramm, *Varieties of Christian Apologetics* (Grand Rapids, MI: Baker, 1961).
[84] Avery Dulles, "The Rebirth of Apologetics," in *Church and Society: The Lawrence*

of all metanarratives and of objective truth itself, many commentators advocate that a revitalization of apologetics will need to appeal to the foundational extra-rational dynamics that make the recognition of credibility and truth possible. For example, Robert Barron asserts that contemporary apologetics must respond to our present radically skeptical age by embracing the "confident use of both the rational and the affective, both the discursive and the intuitive, both the theological and the artistic in the process of bringing people to faith."[85] Newman's apologetics accomplish this synthesis with magnificent aplomb and can inspire others to do the same.

This paper has investigated St. John Henry Newman's apologetic framework and outlined how the interplay between a person's antecedent probabilities, the illative sense, and the accumulation of evidence substantiating the truth claims of Christianity in his writings resulted in an effective defense of the Catholic faith that is simultaneously imaginative, personalist, and intellectual. His profound insights into how one's antecedent probabilities give life to converging strands of evidence and empower one's illative sense to adjudicate truth claims to be credible indicate the crucial role that imaginative and personalist appeals to the heart must play in any system of apologetics. Indeed, Newman's holistic apologetic vision can serve as a model for the ongoing revival and rebirth of apologetics needed in today's world and his works provide us with a generous plethora of imagery, evidence, and cogent arguments for contemporary apologists to incorporate into their own defenses of Catholicism.

Perhaps Mrs. Catherine Froude, one of Newman's dearest friends and a fellow convert, should have the final word on our new saint. Newman and Mrs. Froude, the wife of his close friend William Froude, exchanged letters for many years while she considered following Newman into the Catholic Church. Over time, Newman patiently answered her theological questions, appealed to her antecedent probabilities by encouraging her to deeper prayer, and even offered Masses for her in a personalist appeal for her to

---

J. *McGinley Lectures, 1988–2007* (New York: Fordham University Press, 2008), 441.

[85] Robert Barron, *Exploring Catholic Theology: Essays on God, Liturgy, and Evangelization* (Grand Rapids, MI: Baker Academic, 2015), 92.

recognize where God was leading her. At long last, on March 19, 1857, Catherine Froude was received into the Catholic Church and wrote a heartfelt letter to Newman expressing her profound gratitude and describing the effect of his apologetic approach:

> I know that you will be glad to hear that I was received into the Catholic Church this morning ... I must tell you again how from my heart I thank you for what you have done to help me. Other Catholics always seemed "making a case" when they said things to me,—you always contrived to say exactly what suited my mind.[86]

It would be challenging to find a more beautiful tribute to the value and effectiveness of Newman's framework of apologetics.

When God does not come, He sends. We join together with the universal Church in thanking God for sending us St. John Henry Newman and pray that his apologetic vision may reach an increasingly larger audience in today's world that so desperately needs it and may inspire all to search for and encounter truth.

---

[86] Mrs. Catherine Froude to John Henry Newman (March 19, 1857), in *LD*, XVII, 544.

10

Epilogue

Bishop James Massa

THE CONFERENCE that gave rise to the chapters of this volume was a great gift to our seminary community. It overlapped with the two Feasts of All Saints and All Souls during the year of St. John Henry's canonization. The twofold focus on Newman's personal holiness and the examination of holiness as a topic in his vast corpus invited the participants to trace the remarkable correspondence between his life of heroic virtue and his theological vision. As others have noted, Newman is a saint for our times precisely because, against the increasing cultural marginalization of communities that hold to a biblical orthodoxy and Catholic truth, only a commitment to grow in holiness can sustain the decision of faith. We need Newman more than ever, both the person and his work, in our efforts to form future clergy and lay faithful who can be instruments of sanctification and embodiments of the holiness without which "no one can see God" (Heb 12:14).

I had the privilege of attending both the conference at St. Joseph's Seminary (Dunwoodie) in Yonkers, New York and the earlier celebration in St. Peter's Square on October 13. My seat at the latter event in Rome, among the concelebrating bishops and priests, put me directly underneath the five tapestries of the *Sancti* unfurled over the balcony of the great basilica. Newman's image, based on an 1866 photo, was positioned in the middle of the four women whose lives of holiness differed quite dramatically from his own. Three of these women founded religious congregations of sisters: Mariam Thresia, an Indian mystic devoted to the renewal of family life, Giuseppina Vannini of Italy, and Dulce Lopes Pontes of Brazil, who followed a similar call to care for the sick and poor.

"Heart Speaks to Heart"

The laywoman and seamstress Marguerite Bays received the stigmata after years of charitable works in Switzerland. She died the same year Newman became a cardinal. One can only imagine the delight John Henry has in Heaven as he meets these new friends with whom he shared the earthly honor of being raised to the altar. Both the Victorian man of letters and his four sisters — true contemplatives in action — attest to the diverse charisms found within the communion of saints, each of which plays an essential part in God's great symphony. Each one of these female friends of Christ lived — as Newman most certainly did — "habitually as in the sight of the world to come."

The present volume points to two interlocking themes of friendship and holiness that came up repeatedly in the fall 2019 celebrations of Newman's canonization. Our growth in the likeness of Christ depends in no small way upon the friends that the Lord sends us. St. John Henry has rightfully earned such unofficial titles as "apostle of friendship" and *doctor amicitiae*. He not only teaches us through his sermons, vast correspondences and theological texts how friendship goads the believer toward the truth and ever-deepening holiness, but his own personal journey is a testimony to the indispensable role of friendship in following after the One who went on mission in this world to make of us friends of God (cf. John 15:15).

Newman called his closest friend in life "my earthly light." Ambrose St. John followed the saint into the Catholic Church and lived with him as an Oratorian for more than three decades. The former's death in 1875 brought about an unspeakable sorrow. The intensity of Newman's grief over the loss of Ambrose, beside whom he would be buried, was proportionate to their mutual fraternal love that sustained him through the bitter controversies of his Catholic years. Earlier on, John Henry had found another indispensable friend in Richard Hurrell Froude, who opened up his imagination to the legitimacy of Catholic devotions and Eucharistic Real Presence. Then, there were the women to whom Newman opened up his heart. The artist Maria Giberne followed him into the Catholic Church and left behind portraits of the saint in the Birmingham house. Emily Bowles, who knew Newman at Littlemore, received some of his most forthright criticisms of what he believed was a mistaken path taken by extreme papalists on the issue of infallibility. He looked to friends to air his grievances, to

Epilogue

test his theories and to invite others to enter more deeply into the joy of fellowship he experienced, ultimately as a Catholic priest in the Oratory.

Friendship contains for Newman a power of witness. People come to faith not through rational demonstrations devoid of prior assumptions, but through a preparation of the heart that entails engagement with the testimony of others. In the well-known quote from *Grammar of Assent* cited several times in this volume, Newman captures the essential point about the antecedents brought to bear on demonstrable evidences that allow us to make a right moral judgment or a judgment in favor of the Catholic faith: "The heart is commonly reached, not through reason, but through the imagination, by means of direct impressions, by the testimony of facts and events, by history, by description. Persons influence us, voices melt us, looks subdue us, deeds inflame us."[87] How else did the early Church so effectively win believers to the gospel? Newman answers: "not as a system, not by books, not by argument, nor by temporal power, but by the personal influence of such men … who are at once teachers and the patterns of [a moral power]."[88]

Newman himself was that moral power that awoke many of his fellow Anglicans at Oriel College and St. Mary's Church in Oxford to their Catholic roots. The Oxford Movement depended no less on the "heart to heart" encounters of Newman and his friends than on the arguments of its proponents' tracts. Littlemore, of course, became Newman's lay monastery, a school of consecrated study that, in some ways, eased for him and his companions the transition to Catholicism and anticipated the kind of fraternity he would later discover in the Oratory.

For Newman, friendship plays a crucial role in both evangelization and education. He favored winning souls for Christ "with a line not a net" — that is, one person at a time. He saw friendship between teachers and students as key to cultivating the natural virtues necessary for success in professional life and for expounding Christian doctrine in both faithful continuity with the past and openness to the exigencies of the present. Newman counted on

---

[87] John Henry Newman, *An Essay in Aid of a Grammar of Assent*, edited with Introduction and Notes, I. T. Ker (Oxford: Clarendon Press, 1985), 65–6.

[88] John Henry Newman, *Fifteen Sermons Preached before the University of Oxford between A.D. 1826 and 1843* (London: Longmans, Green and Co, 1909), sermon 5, 92.

invisible friends too in the momentous decisions he took and in the battles he waged. Francis de Sales provided him with a new Catholic framework for the spiritual life. The ancient Fathers taught him how to read the scriptures and understand the Church's oracular role in judging what is in conformity with the Word of God. Philip Neri was his beloved Father of the Oratory, who gave to his priesthood as a Catholic the support of a religious family, a focus on pastoral life and a distinctive example of holiness mixed with joy.

Christians are called to love everyone. Pope Francis, in his encyclical *Fratelli Tutti*, speaks of the need for "social friendship" in our world today. By that term, the Holy Father means an all-inclusive love and fraternity that is co-responsive to people's suffering, regardless of their culture, economic class or political allegiance. Yet, the pope also recognizes that social friendship has its foundation in the family, "where concern and care for others are lived out and handed on." Newman once posed the question whether "the love of many is something superior to the love of one or two." Drawing on the example of the particular love that Jesus showed toward the young apostle John, he answered by saying that "the best preparation for loving the world at large, and loving it duly and wisely, is to cultivate an intimate friendship and affection towards those who are immediately about us."[89] In Newman's mind, we should cultivate lasting and virtue-centered friendships within our homes, our schools and our places of work and recreation, while also putting at their center the One who is "Unchangeable and essentially Good." From these friendships will radiate out an attractive holiness and an active charity that spills over borders and transforms hearts.

A seminary is a good setting for a conference on St. John Henry Newman, for it is above all a school of friendship. For those who participated in the November 1–2, 2019 meeting at Dunwoodie, old friendships were renewed and new ones were made. That should be no surprise, for holiness always attracts. We can be thankful to God that the circle of Newman friends keeps growing in the United States and in other countries to include new generations of seminarians and students of theology. One can only hope that the recognition now given to the English cardinal may lead others to take up his work and be guided by his "kindly light."

---

[89] John Henry Newman, *Parochial and Plain Sermons* (London: Longmans, Green and Co., 1908), II, sermon 5, 52–3.

Index

Abraham 98
Abruzzo 40
Advent 101, 116
Alfieri, Count Vittorio 40, 41
Ambrose, St. 4, 49, 65, 138
Anglicans, Anglicanism, Church of England x, 4, 7, 14, 20, 29, 30, 41, 45, 46, 59, 71, 72, 74, 76, 77, 93, 95, 100, 122, 125
Antichrist 40
Antonucci, Francesco 30
Apollo 6
Aquinas, St. Thomas 4, 19
Aristotle 30, 88, 138
Arnold, Matthew 6
Ascension 114, 115, 118
Athanasius, St. 49, 150
Augustine of Hippo, St. 7, 8, 25, 49
Austen, Jane 93, 94

baptism 4, 64, 73, 97, 112, 116
Barberi, Bl. Dominic 15, 16, 33, 34, 41, 45, 46, 47, 55
Bays, St. Marguerite 156
Bellarmine, Robert 1
Belshazzar 63
Benedict, St. 2, 5, 127
Benedict XVI, Pope 2, 127
Birmingham xi, 20, 54, 83, 150, 156
Bowles, Emily 156
Bozzetti, Giuseppe 50, 51
Buber, Martin 105

Canterbury 100
Capecelatro, Cardinal 41, 42
Capuchins 48
Carlyle, Thomas 22
Castro Giovanni 43, 55
Catholic Faith Network 12
Catholic University of Ireland 17

Chalcedon, Council of 3
Chesterton, G. K. 19, 31, 32
Chiesa Nuova 54
Christie, John Frederic 42
Christmas 101
Church, Richard 94, 95
Collegio Rosmini 49
Cristoforo, Fra 48, 49

Dalgairns, J. D. 44, 49, 50, 51, 53, 132
Darnall Hall, Sheffield 18
Davidson, Sean 29
Davis, Huw Twiston 33
Decrees and encyclicals
  Ad Gentes 4
  Amoris Laetitia 30, 64, 65, 66
  Apostolicam Actuositatem 2, 4
  Dei Verbum 1, 5
  Evangelii Gaudium 64, 66
  Familiaris Consortio 67
  Fides et Ratio 51
  Fratelli Tutti 158
  Gaudium et Spes 2, 4, 5
  Laudato Sí 105
  Lumen Gentium 1, 4
  Nostra Aetate 2, 5
  Pascendi Dominici Gregis 84
  Sacrosanctum Concilium 5
  Unitatis Redintegratio 2
Descartes, René 105, 136
Dessain, Charles Stephen 17, 40, 54, 72, 126, 137
Dominic, St. 5, 15, 16, 33
Dublin 18, 83, 122
du Boulay, Sr. Mary Gabriel 129, 130
Dunwoodie xi, 11, 12, 155, 158

Easter 115, 122

Eden 42
Etna 55
Eucharist, Mass xi, 5, 11, 12, 13, 57, 64, 65, 66, 67, 68, 76, 80, 112, 113, 121, 122, 123, 124

Faber, F. W. 54
Florence 54
Fourdrinier, Jemima 19
Francis de Sales, St. 33, 158
Francis of Assisi, St. 19
Francis, Pope xi, 14, 30, 64, 65, 66, 67, 68, 105, 158
Froude, Anthony James 21, 22, 23, 96, 152, 153, 156
Froude, Catherine 152
Froude, Hurrell 22, 96, 156

Gainford, R. J. 18
Galilee 115
Gennaro 43
Ghianda (chaplain) 49
Giberne, Maria 156
Gladstone, William 6
Gregory I, Pope (St. Gregory the Great) 150
Gregory VII, Pope St. 150

Hampden, Renn Dickson 59, 95, 96
Hawkins, Edward, provost of Oriel College 21
Hügel, Baron von 30
Huguenots 19
Hume, David 134, 135, 146

Ignatius of Loyola, St. 5, 29

Jerusalem 13, 33, 73
John Paul II, Pope St. xi, 51, 67
Joubert, Joseph 87
Judea 115

Kant, Immanuel 83, 85, 88, 105
Kaspar, Walter 30–1, 66
Ker, Ian xi, xii, xvi, xvii, xx, 1–10, 39, 40–1, 72, 93, 94, 95, 101, 116, 127, 137, 139, 143, 144, 149

Kingsley, Charles 20, 126
Kuhn, Thomas 31

Leo XIII, Pope x, 20, 108, 126
Liguori, St. Alfonso 41, 44, 45, 55
Littlemore 15, 46, 56, 156, 157
Loughborough 49
Lopes Pontes, St. Dulce 155

Manzoni, Alessandro 41, 47, 48, 49, 50, 51, 55, 56
Marcel, Gabriel 105
Mariam Thresia, St. 155
Mary Magdalen, St. 29
Milan 27, 49, 51, 56
Monica, St. 49

Naples 43, 45
Natural Religion 110, 148
Neo-Platonism 70, 71
Neri, Philip, St. 5, 29, 41, 52, 54, 55, 158
Newman, Charles 131
Newman, Jemima 47
Newman, St. John Henry
An Essay on the Development of Doctrine 35
Apologia pro Vita Sua x, 15, 20, 26, 29, 41, 44, 94, 95, 100, 108, 112, 126, 132, 147, 149
Biglietto Address x, xii, 20, 55, 90, 108, 126
Callista 6, 7, 10, 69, 70, 71, 143
Certain Difficulties Felt by Anglicans 6, 58, 77, 143
Cor ad cor loquitur xi, 33, 82, 105, 144
Discourses Addressed to Mixed Congregations 28, 37, 62, 63
Essay in Aid of a Grammar of Assent 77, 78, 81, 105, 106, 109, 110, 137, 138, 139, 140, 142, 143, 147, 148, 157
Essay on the Development of Christian Doctrine 2, 3, 4, 35, 146, 147
Essay on the Development of Doctrine 35, 53

Index

Lectures on Justification 107, 112, 113, 114
Letter to the Duke of Norfolk 5, 77
Loss and Gain 143, 144
Meditation on God's Providence 51
Oxford University Sermons 60, 61, 71, 73, 74, 107, 109, 110, 112, 132, 133, 134, 145, 146, 157
Parochial and Plain Sermons vii, x, xi, 7, 14, 18, 29, 30, 39, 57, 59, 71, 94, 114, 158
The Idea of a University 34, 58, 59, 94
Two Essays on Biblical and Ecclesiastical Miracles 146
Newman, Mary 19
Nicene Creed 91

Old Catholic Church 3
Oriel College, Oxford 1, 21, 133, 157
Oxford Movement x, 4, 5, 81, 82, 94, 95, 96, 100, 101, 157

Palermo 43
Paley, William 133
Pascal, Blaise 106
Passionists 15, 45, 47
Pattison, Mark 21
Paul, St. 13, 27, 40, 64, 66, 95, 98, 109, 113, 117, 118
Perrone, Giovanni 41, 52, 53, 54, 55, 133
phronesis 88, 138
Pius IX, Pope Bl. 1, 47
  Syllabus of Errors 1
Pius X, Pope St. 84
Propaganda, College of 52
Pym, Barbara 40

Ratcliffe College 49, 50

Reding, Charles 144
Reform Bill 94
Rockville Centre xii, 12
Rogers, Frederic 48
Rosminians 49, 50
Rosmini, Bl. Antonio 41, 49, 50, 51, 55
Russell, Charles 44

Simeon, Louisa 140
Sladen, Douglas 43
St. Bernard's Seminary 150
Steiner, George 121, 123
Stewart, James 17
St. John, Ambrose 29, 44, 50, 52, 156
St. Mary's Church, Oxford 100, 157
Synthetic Society 85, 86, 87, 88, 90

Taormina 42
Taylor, Charles 123
Thompson, Francis 91
Trevor, Meriol 40
Trollope, Anthony 95
Tyrrell, George 30

Ultramontanism 3

Vaccari, Msgr. 12
Vannini, St. Giuseppina 155
Vatican I 3, 6
Vatican II xii, 1, 2, 3, 4, 5, 6, 109
Velocci, Giovanni 45
Vestivo, Luigi 43

Ward, Wilfred 82, 84, 85, 86, 87, 88, 89, 90, 91, 92
Whately, Richard 95, 133

Xavier, St. Francis, 46